COACHING, COUNSELING & MENTORING

COACHING, COUNSELING & MENTORING

How to Choose & Use the Right Technique to Boost Employee Performance

Florence M. Stone

American Management Association

New York • Atlanta • Boston • Chicago • Kansas City • San Francisco • Washington, D.C.
Brussels • Mexico City • Tokyo • Toronto

*This publication is designed to provide accurate and authoritative
information in regard to the subject matter covered. It is sold with
the understanding that the publisher is not engaged in rendering
legal, accounting, or other professional service. If legal advice or
other expert assistance is required, the services of a competent professional person should be sought.*

Library of Congress Cataloging-in-Publication Data

Stone, Florence M.
    *Coaching, counseling & mentoring : how to choose & use the right
technique to boost employee performance / Florence M. Stone.*
        p. cm.
    Includes index.
    ISBN 0-8144-0416-2
    *1. Mentoring in business. 2. Employees—Counseling of.
3. Employees—Training of.   I. Title.*
HF5385.S76   1998
658.3'124—dc21   *98-35081*
                                                              CIP

Printing number

10   9   8   7   6   5

To my dad,
Edward John Arthur Stone

Contents

COACHING, COUNSELING & MENTORING

Introduction

If your organization is to sustain its competitive advantage, it needs employees who are productive and willing to continually learn and adapt as their roles change along with the organization. Today's companies need people who at best exceed expectations and at worst meet standards. Managers with good people skills can get that kind of performance from their employees by using the tools of coaching, counseling, and mentoring. Because it means better bottom-line results, organizations recognize and reward such managers. Being a good coach, counselor, and mentor could be your ticket to advancement.

Now, with escalating time pressures and constant change, upper management is on the lookout for managers who can recruit capable employees, develop the skills they need to do today's jobs, and prepare them to handle tomorrow's jobs as well; who recognize their obligation to confront poor performers and who will work with these people to find a solution or make the tough decisions to terminate those who are dragging down the rest of the team; and who can keep their superstars shining even when there is little opportunity for advancement or dollars for increased performance.

In short, organizations want and reward managers who are skilled at the managerial tasks of coaching, counseling, and mentoring. Note that they are referred to here as "managerial responsibilities" and with good reason; coaching, counseling, and mentoring, while people-oriented, are very much a part of a manager's job—and have always been so. The demands on organizations, however, have made them critical skills today. Which is why this book has been developed. It not only describes each responsibility but when to use which and how to most effectively use it—something many managers aren't always sure about.

Clearing Up the Mystery

Confusion about these three skills abounds. A review of the management literature would suggest that the confusion is only semantic, with coaching confused with counseling, coaching confused with mentoring, and mentoring confused with coaching and counseling. But the confusion goes deeper. All managers pay lip service to them, many managers think they are good at them, but very few managers are skilled at doing them. Managers and team leaders may have a general idea about how to coach, how to counsel, and/or how to mentor someone, but for the most part they are unaware of the various roles involved in each task or the best way of proceeding. Nor do they know all the problems they may encounter if they don't do it right.

In this book you will find answers to all the questions you might have about coaching, counseling, and mentoring, including the traps you could fall into and, more important, how to avoid them.

What's the Difference Between Coaching, Counseling, and Mentoring?

To help you get the terminology straight, in this book the term *coaching* refers to continually developing employees so that they do their jobs well. Comparable to the work of a professional coach, managerial coaching involves not only assessment of development needs and subsequent training but also making good hires to begin with. Good coaches recruit only the best, and they train newcomers to close whatever skill gaps remain and more experienced workers to update their skills and increase their employability. You should also communicate organization values and mission to ensure that your staff is prepared to be empowered and even to share your leadership responsibilities.

There are mistakes you can make along the way, mistakes that

& consulting

can take a capable newcomer and turn her into a troublesome employee, or an employee with a personal problem into a problem employee. Either situation would demand *counseling*, defined here as a four-step process, of which one-on-one communications are most important since the success of these meetings could mean the difference between an employee's continued employment or not.

The hard work of your team can be undone by just one employee who doesn't carry his weight. Consequently, poor performance can't be tolerated. Employees who are working ineffectively need to know it, and they need your help to make the necessary improvements. In today's tough antidiscrimination legal climate, you need to be able to demonstrate as well that you have expended every reasonable effort to help employees perform well. You should have documentation to show that a suspended or discharged employee was warned and that help was available. This book will show you how to conduct effective counseling sessions, with written records of these sessions and with an action plan, the necessary evidence you will need should an aggrieved employee take legal action against your organization.

Some managers think they can avoid counseling traps just by ignoring performance problems, but that can be the biggest career mistake of all, should litigation result from this failure.

Whereas counseling is concerned with your poorer performers, *mentoring* is directed to your best performers. You become role model, coach, broker, and advocate for your outstanding performers to sustain their motivation despite limited opportunities for advancement, as well as to give them opportunities to utilize their abilities both to their own benefit and that of the organization. Besides the personal satisfaction and pride you feel in helping one of your staff members grow, you will have someone who can take on important projects or assume some of your mundane tasks, which will in turn free you to take on more rewarding, high-visibility projects.

Done right, mentoring one employee can motivate not only that person but also the remainder of your staff as you demonstrate that you truly care about your people. On the other hand, mentoring, if done incorrectly, can create jealousies, suspicion about motive, charges of discrimination, and many more troubles.

How This Book Is Organized

Section I of this book is devoted to coaching, Section II to counseling, and Section III to mentoring. The first chapter in each section provides an overview of the managerial process. The second chapter zeroes in on one critical element of the process to ensure that you maximize its benefits.

Each section recognizes that you now manage not only individual employees but teams—either groups of individuals from throughout the organization or members of your own department—so there is a separate chapter on how you can apply the process in a group environment, from team coaching to team counseling to team sponsorship.

In the fourth and final chapter in each section, the book comes to grips with those traps and problems associated with the process.

What's in It for Me

Since you picked up this book, I have to assume that you either have a specific problem with an employee and hope that you can find a solution within its pages or you suspect that your department could be more productive than it is and hope that you will find ways to boost the output of your average staff members, turn your good employees into better ones, and transform your best workers into superperformers.

Whichever the reason, you should find the answer here. Better, when you succeed in effectively applying this trio of processes, creating your own total performance management process, and you boost your employees' performance, you will find you get the attention from upper management your people management efforts merit.

Some Cases in Point

To demonstrate just how valuable the advice in this book can be to your department's or team's productivity, let me share with you ten people situations. Very likely, you've encountered several; if you haven't, you probably know of someone in your organization who has. They're the people situations that continually frustrate and can burn out managers today. In this book, you'll discover the answers that will enable you to handle them confidently the next time or, better yet, prevent their recurrence.

Situation 1. Luanne, a company programmer, has been absent almost one day every week. She keeps complaining about the stress associated with the work. When you bring up the problem with her, she attributes it to the increase in her workload and argues that she needs at least one day off each week as a "reasonable accommodation" under the Americans with Disabilities Act. You explain that you would then have to hire a temp to work on the day she is absent, which is economically prohibitive. You believe that, together, you need to identify some alternative solutions to the stress she believes is a part of her job. But she refuses to discuss any other alternatives. *What would you do?*

Situation 2. Laura is hiring a new artist for the printing shop. She has limited her choice to two candidates. Both have held the same job titles, but Julio has worked in more structured organizations in the past and has all the skills needed for the job. Henrietta, on the other hand, lacks some skills critical to the job, but she is used to the kind of team-oriented operation you run. *What would you do?*

Situation 3. Arlene is one of your fastest data entry operators when you keep at her. In crises, she also pulls herself together and gets everything done. But if you ease off, focusing on your own work rather than constantly monitoring her performance, she begins to fiddle with her hair or pull out a book and let the work sit on her desk. She's been on warning twice, but each time, after her performance improved, she was taken off warning. *What would you do?*

Situation 4. Darrell disagreed with a decision made at a team meeting and stomped out. It wasn't the first time he had acted childishly when an idea he had proposed failed to get the agreement of the team. The members have asked you to take him off the team; they believe his temper tantrums are creating an uncreative environment. On the other hand, you know that Darrell, at his best, is one of the most creative members of the team. *What would you do?*

Situation 5. Nick is one of your best employees, but he's been moping since you announced that a pet project of his would have to be discontinued. There are other projects he could oversee, but there are some people skills he lacks that are important to the success of these initiatives. *What would you do?*

Situation 6. Bill's performance appraisal review is not going well. You have some specific subjects you want to discuss, yet he keeps chattering about this situation or that, almost as if he suspects that you have some problems with his performance that you want to discuss. *What would you do?*

Situation 7. Maxine has the potential to take on much more work than she currently does, at least you believe so, but right now her output ranges from poor to average. You realize that the job is pretty monotonous for someone with her experience—she had been transferred from another department to avoid downsizing her—and the current position is much simpler than the one she previously held. *What would you do?*

Situation 8. Linda, a manager, is being pressured by her boss to put Sylvia, one of Linda's staff members, on warning. Tom doesn't like Sylvia's attitude. Sylvia is a loner, uncomfortable in team settings. And Tom feels that she should speak up more at meetings and, given her three years with the organization, should have more knowledge about the organization than she does. Linda doesn't agree with Tom's concerns. She knows about and can document some problems with Sylvia's performance, and she could use those to justify putting Sylvia on warning, but other employees with similar problems first went through counseling. Tom doesn't want to waste the time; he wants Sylvia out and someone who better fits the company's new culture in her place. *What would you do?*

Situation 9. Andrea, a customer service rep, lost her temper with customers on several occasions and consequently was placed in counseling. She continues to have problems with customers on the phone, but today you observed her helping an older customer with a billing problem when she took over the front customer desk.

Her behavior was quite unusual for her: She was patient and considerate with the customer. This incident stands out because it shows that she could develop the right behavior. On the other hand, this one incident seems insignificant when weighed against the three or four phone calls in which you heard her snap at callers. *What would you do?*

Situation 10. Blair is in before 9 A.M. and stays later than 5 P.M. At meetings, she seems very much in charge of her work. Her co-workers respect her and, a long-time employee, she has numerous good friends among your staff members. Which is all great. Except, as Blair's supervisor, you are familiar with her work, and you know that she spends a considerable amount of the workday on the phone or visiting with friends. Her work is full of errors and, despite your conversations with her, there has been no real effort to improve. She blames the problem on your failure to communicate instructions clearly and be explicit about her job priorities. *What would you do?*

If you want to solve problems like these, you have to understand whether coaching, counseling, or mentoring is called for and how best to use the technique. That way, not only can you solve the specific dilemma but you can move beyond it to continue performance improvement. And win management's recognition.

Section I
COACHING

Chapter 1
Getting Started

Coaching is the process by which employees gain the skills, abilities, and knowledge they need to develop themselves professionally and become more effective in their jobs. When you coach your employees, you increase both their performance in their current jobs and their potential to do more in the future.

Coaching is designed to boost performance levels by making clear to employees what they should do and how they should best do it (think "instruction"), positively reinforce good work (think "praise"), and find ways to redesign employees' jobs or increase their contribution (think "empowerment" or "shared leadership").

But increased employee performance isn't the sole benefit of your coaching. When employees receive regular feedback from you, you won't have to worry about their being surprised and defensive at performance appraisal time. And the rapport between you and your employees that coaching creates should help reduce complaints from employees. Everything should run more smoothly—or, at least, as well as it can in today's leaner organizations in which crisis management is often the order of the day. Certainly, you won't have to worry so much about getting demerits from senior management for people problems.

Instead, upper management will likely recognize your people skills. While it might seem that people skills don't get the attention they deserve, so long as they result in high productivity, which translates into decreased operating costs or increased income, then coaching can enhance your reputation.

Your Beliefs About People

Coaching begins with an assumption: Most employees are eager to do well, to please their managers, and to achieve as high a position as they can with the company. As coach, you can ensure that your employees do all three.

Should this approach to performance management be contrary to your own mind-set about your employees—that is, should you believe that, on the contrary, your employees don't care about their work, have no interest in pleasing you, and are quite happy going nowhere in their careers—then you may want to stop reading this section of the book and proceed to Section II, on counseling. Better still, continue to read.

Motivational research conducted by psychologist Abraham Maslow and others shows that most people have a genuine interest in bettering themselves and in achieving all that they can be. You don't have to threaten or force employees to get them to increase their performance so long as you give them reason to do so. You don't have to offer financial rewards or promotions. By giving your employees the opportunity to increase their employability by offering them assignments and providing training to help them grow beyond their current positions, and by creating the kind of environment in which your employees feel free to share their ideas and then get recognition for those ideas and their efforts to implement them, you are contributing to that sense of job satisfaction that can increase job performance.

And managers who show a willingness to coach their employees toward realizing their full potential and building their confidence gain their employees' loyalty and respect. If you doubt the worth of this statement, what do you think is the value of the following?

◇ Employees who are oriented to corporate values and business intent and strategies

◇ Employees who are clear about your expectations for their performance and their priorities

◇ Employees who accept responsibility for their performance and are motivated to exceed their current performance

These benefits, too, come from coaching.

Managerial Resistance

Many managers argue that they don't have the time to coach. But coaching is not time-intensive; rather, the problems from not coaching can become time-intensive. If you don't continually work at developing your employees' skills, much of the additional work in your leaner organization will wind up on your shoulders.

Another reason managers give for not coaching is that their employees don't need the added attention; they already know what is expected of them. But ask yourself, "How little will it cost me to confirm this by assuming the role of coach in meetings with my employees?" Or, put another way, "How much will it cost me if I am wrong and my employees truly don't have a clear idea of my expectations or priorities?"

Still another excuse of managers for not coaching is that their employees should take responsibility for their own development and careers. Yes, employees *are* ultimately responsible for their development and careers. But managers' helping to increase their employees' employability has two benefits: It can better prepare employees to take on more responsibility, and simultaneously it helps build loyalty. Efforts at training employees beyond the level of their current jobs have been found to build greater employee commitment to corporate values and mission as well as a better relationship between employee and supervisor.

The Five Principles of Coaching

To fulfill your responsibilities as a coach, there are some definite skills you need. These are the same skills the best sports coaches have. And they are important whether you are coaching a group or an individual player:

1. *Gathering information.* A good coach knows how to get information from an individual without making that person feel as if he or she is being interrogated. Such information is important in making numerous decisions, ranging from whether to hire a particular job candidate to identifying a skill deficiency or the existence of any confusion about how to do a particular job, to finding out an employee's interests and aspirations so as to redesign his or her job and thereby stimulate above-standard performance.

2. *Listening.* Asking the right questions means little if you don't listen to the replies. A good coach is able to listen with a "third ear," paying as much attention to the nonverbal signals and body posture of the speaker as to his or her words in order to determine the feelings behind the response as well as its truthfulness. That same coach also knows how to use body language to communicate interest in what the speaker has to say.

3. *Being aware of what's happening around you.* You should talk frequently to your employees to see if there are morale problems or other causes of distress in the workplace that could lower productivity or generate attitudinal problems or, better, signs that an employee is not only willing but ready and able to assume more responsibility. Let's see how one coach keeps the lines of communication open.

Adrienne's "Open-Door" Policy

Adrienne is good at coaching, although the terms *manager* and *leader* are more often used to describe her strong points. Still, Adrienne is a coach in that she meets weekly with her team of copywriters to discuss progress on marketing assignments and to share with her team compliments from her boss and others in the organization about the fine work they are doing. But Adrienne doesn't limit her communications with her staff to these group meetings.

Adrienne's staff members know that all they need do is to knock on her door to get time with her to discuss a work problem or even a personal problem. Adrienne will also often stop at people's desks to chat about some project or other they are completing. Her goal is to gather information about any problems they are encountering—

either because of skill gaps they have or difficulties within the very political consumer products company in which they work.

Such information, then, can become the basis for her one-on-one monthly meetings with each of her staff members, in which she talks about concerns either she or the employee has about the work getting done. Sometimes these sessions lead to the registration of a staff member in a training program to develop his skills; sometimes they identify the need for a meeting among Adrienne, the staff member, and the product manager to be sure that the copywriting department and product management are both reading from the same page; and sometimes these meetings simply enable her to tell an employee just how fine a job he is doing. Whatever the result, Adrienne considers them valuable because they keep her in touch with her staff's needs (including the need for an occasional pat on the back), something that might not happen, given the many work distractions in the office, if these exchanges were less formalized.

4. *Instructing employees.* A good coach is able to train employees, either singly or in a group. Even before that, he or she is able to conduct a training needs assessment to determine gaps in knowledge that must be filled. (For more on this subject, see Chapter 2).

5. *Giving feedback.* A good coach knows how important feedback is in improving the performance of an employee. There is no such thing as too little time to provide praise for a job well done or to provide corrective feedback, including suggestions for improvement that tell the employee that the manager believes that he or she is capable of doing the work right. In short, a good coach doesn't allow today's lean organizations to provide an excuse for not positively reinforcing good work or not providing corrective feedback in a positive manner.

The Duties of a Coach

The term *coach* is associated with on-the-job training, but the role of coach involves more than training, albeit that is a part of the responsibility. Besides training, as coach you are responsible for:

◇ Acting as a role model for higher performance.
◇ Hiring the best.
◇ Creating a work culture in which employees have reason to be motivated.
◇ Clarifying expectations—both micro expectations associated with particular jobs and macro objectives tied to the organization's overall strategy and mission.
◇ Providing feedback on your employees' behavior that will put them on the right performance track and keep them there.
◇ Applying the performance evaluation process not only as a measurement tool tied to raises but also as a developmental aid.
◇ Providing the training and resources employees need to improve their performance.
◇ Praising, praising, and praising some more to reinforce positive performance.

Let's look at these in greater depth:

Acting as a Role Model

Many managers see a coach solely in the sports context—as a Knute Rockne who calls the staff together and gives pep talks. Yes, this is part of being a coach, but there is much more. Certainly a managerial coach should be supportive and nurturing, ready with know-how to help employees succeed in their jobs and with recognition when they do. But managerial coaches, unlike their sports equivalents, are on the field from the start of the workday to its end, five days a week, like their players, and they should be role models for their players.

You probably remember the axiom "Do what I say, not what I do." As a managerial coach, you don't want your staff members to snicker and attribute such a phrase to you. For instance, you can't tell your employees that honesty is important in their reports to you about progress on their work yet lie yourself to senior management about the department's quarterly results. Or you might talk to your work team about the importance of customer service, inside and outside the organization, yet be known as the one manager who never returns customer calls. One employee told me about her manager who was forever ranting about expecting everyone at their desks by 9 A.M.; yet this manager would too frequently stroll into the office after 9:30. She always had a reason—from transportation foul-ups to late nights working at home—and her reasons might even have been legitimate, but over time, as her behavior belied her words, her message about punctuality became an office joke.

You have to recognize that when you are in the field (to continue with the sports metaphor), your staff will be watching your plays *and* emulating them. Be sure that they are plays that you would want to see emulated.

One other point: Don't make promises to employees if you don't plan to keep them. Be particularly wary of promises to maintain open and honest communications, to provide each employee with the opportunity to reach his or her potential, the opportunity for empowerment, and recognition and reward for excellence and outstanding performance. Your credibility is important to successful coaching.

Hiring the Best

Yes, in a sense, coaching begins even before someone is on staff as you select those individuals who have the job skills and experience and, maybe most important of all, the potential to move up beyond the current job.

You want to hire for your department individuals who would fit this profile:

◇ They are continually in search of more knowledge and are eager to develop new skills.
◇ They won't accept the current way of doing things. They have their own ideas and challenge existing practices.
◇ They want to know the whys and wherefores of things. In keeping with their desire to find more efficient or effective ways of doing their work, they won't accept anything without explanation.
◇ They are restless and dissatisfied if they don't have challenges. If they have finished their own work, they are the

employees who offer a helping hand to coworkers or to their boss.

Creating the Right Climate

To be successful in your role as coach, you will need to create a climate that contributes to a free and open exchange of ideas and is seen as a learning environment by your employees. Your goal is to create an energizing environment that stimulates employees' internal motivation to produce.

You create such an environment by:

◇ *Keeping threats, even implied ones, out of your conversations.* For instance, never say to an employee, "If you, Phil, want to succeed in this job, you had better. . . ." Or, worse, "Debbie, if you want to *keep* your job, you had better. . . ." Such comments are seen as implied or overt threats and will be met with denial, flight, or anger, all responses that can undermine the time you spend training Phil or Debbie to use their full potential.

◇ *Building rapport with your employees.* I'm not suggesting that you lunch daily with your employees or go for drinks after work. But you should demonstrate a caring attitude toward your employees, a willingness to put aside the stack of papers on your desk to discuss personal problems as well as work-related ones. A manager earns the trust of his employees by demonstrating an honest interest in them and fostering open and candid two-way communication. And a wise manager keeps their problems confidential.

◇ *Developing a flexible management style.* Just as you wouldn't use the same management style for every situation you confront, you should not use the same style in working with the diverse members of your work group. Employees are individuals with individual needs. As a manager, you should treat all your employees fairly but not necessarily the same. For instance, an employee who is new will need more direction than a more experienced employee. Likewise, a five-year veteran in the department who is taking on a new responsibility will need more direction than another five-year veteran who is doing the same routine work she has been doing for the past five years.

◇ *Supporting an employee's effort.* When you are discussing skill gaps or the need for additional training or other developmental needs, you want to come across as a cheerleader, not as an evaluator. You want your remarks to be perceived as helpful feedback rather than as criticism. Keep in mind that the phrase *constructive criticism* is an oxymoron. Provide constructive feedback instead. Keep your remarks upbeat, pointing to both those things your employee has done right and to those things he did wrong. And end your comments with a statement that reassures your employee that you have confidence in his ability to do the task well or to complete the assignment on schedule or to learn how to use the newest software program.

◇ *Looking at mistakes as learning opportunities.* You should point to a problem and tell the employee, "Okay, this isn't working. What can we learn from our approach here?" The message you are sending to the employee is that mistakes can be valuable for teaching us, supporting your desire to create a learning environment. The employee won't be frightened to test out her ideas because she will know that you recognize that not all efforts will be successful—in short, that there is failure associated with risk, but that mistakes do not mean that the risk taker is a failure.

◇ *Separating the behavior from the person.* You want the employee to come away from the coaching with his or her self-esteem intact. Let's say that you have a member of your work team who dominates the discussion. In coaching him, you might tell the individual, "You often have good ideas, Sam, but we lose others' ideas when you monopolize the team discussions." Sam will leave the meeting with you feeling that his effort is appreciated but aware that his behavior needs to be changed, and he should learn to listen as much as talk at staff meetings.

◇ *Recognizing improvement.* Just as you don't want to destroy an employee's self-esteem by criticizing her behavior or some work she has done, you also want to build up her self-esteem. When she has made an effort to improve her performance, this staff member's self-esteem and efforts to continue improving can be increased by your acknowledgement of the improvements. Even small improvements should be recognized since such feedback can stimulate the employee to work on greater changes.

◇ *Building on strengths and assets.* You can energize employees by letting them know that you recognize their strengths. It doesn't matter if you know that Carol occasionally is careless, or comes in late, or has a hard time writing proposals. When Carol completes a vendor comparison and comes up with several ways to save the department money, it's important to communicate to her how much her efforts are appreciated. After this, Carol certainly will be more amenable to discussing with you her tardiness or carelessness and to taking instruction from you on how to put together better proposals.

Clarifying Expectations and Providing Feedback

If there is one situation that can keep your department from attaining a high level of performance, it is confusion among your employees about your expectations. You need to be specific not only about the tasks that have to be done and the order of priorities for assignments but also about the game plan for the team. That game plan is made up of several elements:

◇ *Department mission and operating goals.* Ideally, these should have been developed with the group. But periodically you should also remind the staff about them, perhaps in regular status reports about progress toward achieving them.

◇ *Corporate strategy and mission.* If you want to get the most from your employees, you need to let them know as much as possible about the bigger corporate picture. That includes information about the company's financial position. Whether news is good or bad, knowing the situation is better than speculating.

◇ *Corporate values.* Your staff should know what initiatives senior management has identified to help the company achieve a competitive advantage. Don't just read the list, as written by top management. Discuss with your team how these values translate into behaviors that are a part of members' jobs.

When employees know these values and have a clear idea about their role in the bigger picture, they are better prepared to understand and accept the job feedback you give them, even when it is negative. Here's how to make that feedback valuable:

◇ *Plan what you will say.* This ensures that you don't allow any personal frustration to creep into your remarks.

◇ *Be patient.* What may be very simple to you because you have done this kind of work for many years may not be so simple to someone who is doing it for the first time. In time, with your help, an employee might even find a more efficient way to do the same work that you are currently concerned about his or her ability to master.

◇ *Be specific, not general.* You want the individual to have enough details to be able to make specific changes in his behavior. It's not enough, for instance, to tell an employee to "think more globally." Rather, you can suggest that you want him "to stay in touch with co-workers in our European subsidiary—we need to be alert to synergistic opportunities. We missed out on signing a contract with that multinational because we didn't know that our European division had contacts with its British executive director." Or, rather than tell an employee to be "more customer-focused," you should tell her, "I was disappointed that we haven't done a customer focus group this quarter. If we are to stay abreast of our customers' needs, we need to hold these meetings at least quarterly."

◇ *Be descriptive, not evaluative.* Again, you should be very specific about the situation, not just judgmental. Let's assume that one of your staff members did a poor job meeting and greeting some potential clients yesterday. Instead of telling him, "You really messed up yesterday," you should tell him, "You need to do your homework before clients visit. You didn't know. . . ."

◇ *Be sensitive to your feelings at the time.* You may destroy the rapport you have built with an employee if you give her feedback at a moment when you are angry. The temptation to relieve your own frustration by blaming this person may be great, but it's a temptation that you should resist. The short-term satisfaction could have long-term repercussions as you destroy the relationship between you and this employee.

◇ *Use words, body language, and tone of voice to show that your intention is to help.* You want your employee to listen to your feedback, even if it is critical of his or her performance. Your communication style will make a difference.

◇ *Focus on behavior that can be changed.* You will only frustrate your employees by identifying shortfalls over which they have no control. To keep from falling into this trap, never make assumptions about situations. Begin any discussion about some work undone or finished behind schedule by asking "who," "what," "where," and "how." Note that I haven't suggested that you use "why" questions; they can easily put an individual on the defensive. "Why" questions are best saved for follow-up to get more insight after you have a clearer idea of a situation's cause.

◇ *Show how the job should be done.* You don't only describe how the work was done wrong; where it is possible, you should also show how it should be done. It isn't enough to tell an employee, "You goofed. Try again, maybe next time you'll get it right."

◇ *Listen to the employee's explanation.* Sometimes you will get an excuse. But there may also be plausible reasons for a problem that you aren't aware of. If so, say, "Thank you."

◇ *Give your employee some extra time.* You know you have to give constructive feedback, pointing up those aspects of the work that were especially well done to ensure their repetition, as well as noting faults in a job done. But once you have given feedback, don't just walk away from the employee. Give the employee a little personal time to share with you why he did the job as it was done. Wouldn't you want some extra time to explain your success and bond with your supervisor after she said you did well?

Applying the Performance Appraisal as a Developmental Tool

Employee evaluations are perfect opportunities for you to put on your coaching hat and discuss ways in which your employees can improve their work. Many managers forget the developmental side of evaluations. Good appraisals don't only assess employees' performance; they also identify opportunities for improvement.

Too often at the end of an appraisal year, managers talk only about the rating for the past year and its fiscal consequences. Instead, in your coaching role you should be laying the groundwork for next year's performance appraisal by discussing an employee development plan that addresses problem areas that kept the individual from achieving his or her outcomes in the past year.

Such development plans are as important to your high performers as they are to your average or poor performers. If an employee has consistently exceeded standards and done so for several years, she is probably frustrated by the lack of opportunities for promotion or new challenges. This is the time, then, to discuss training programs she can use to develop skills that could lead to advancement, in other words, to increasing her employability.

The end-of-year meeting isn't the only time during the year that you can address these issues. At every quarterly review, you might want to work out development programs with employees to minimize any shortcomings that are likely to cause them to fall behind in the goals set for the year.

In the next chapter, the role of appraisals in coaching will be discussed in greater detail, as one of two ways to add stretch to your employees' performance. The other technique involves conducting training assessments. The key is to create development plans for your employees.

Taking on Your Developmental Responsibilities

You help your employees to grow professionally by reviewing their job descriptions in order to define the core competencies of their jobs. With this information, you can then determine if each job holder possesses these competencies or not. A competency is a skill, ability, area of knowledge, set of experiences, or attitude, and it is a manager's responsibility, in his or her role as coach, to determine if there are any competencies lacking in the members of the team. This kind of assessment is done, first, by breaking down each competency into specific behaviors, then by observing staff members at work to see what they can and cannot do.

The findings then become the basis of developmental plans for staff members. Successful plans focus on no more than two or three areas for development and contain specific time frames for accomplishment. Of course, each skill or area of knowledge should be well defined. Within the plan, too, the means for developing that skill or knowledge area should be spelled out. It makes no sense, for instance, to create a development plan for an employee that has her attending night school to become more proficient in some new office technology when there are no funds to pay for the training.

The developmental plan need not involve off-site training. An employee can grow in his job with customized assignments, ranging from such simple ones as completing a self-development tape or acting as a buddy to a newcomer to more complex ones like being given a temporary lateral transfer or asked to attend a conference, to those with great stretch like working with mergers, acquisitions, or new divisions that are growing to improve business results or working with a cross-functional group at an offshore location.

Where a development plan calls for you to act as a trainer yourself, you should:

◇ *Present the big picture.* Your employees know their jobs, but they may not know how they contribute to the bigger corporate picture. Let them know their role's influence on the company's strategic direction if there is one.

◇ *Provide sufficient time for an employee to develop the new skill.* We all seem to be on our own personal treadmills. But you can't expect your employees to learn new skills or acquire added capabilities overnight. So any training effort should provide enough time for mastering the learning.

◇ *Start from where the employee currently is.* Don't overwhelm the employee in providing instruction, but also don't treat her as incompetent because of her need for training. Treat the person as a competent human being who has proven to be a successful learner in the past and can absorb this new training as well.

◇ *Present your instruction in the form of a problem to be solved.* This may actually be the case where the training is designed to fill a knowledge or skill gap. Let's say that you have an employee who does less than well in making a critical presentation to a client. If you don't want the incident to be repeated, you have to meet with the employee, provide feedback about his performance that is constructive, and together decide on how he is to perfect the capability, whether it is part of the employee's current job or represents an expansion of his responsibilities and the potential for advancement.

◇ *Find a place that is free from interruptions in which to do your training.* Set aside at least an hour, but no more than two hours because employees can become too fatigued to absorb instructions over a longer time span.

◇ *Demonstrate the desired outcome.* The employee has to know why the work is to be done as you instruct. Taking him through the process to completion should help make that clear. While the employee may identify over time a more effective or efficient way to do the same work, initially you want your worker to follow your instructions carefully.

When you show someone how to perform a task, the training should approximate the conditions of the job. Use the actual equipment and, ideally, install the equipment in a space similar to that in which it will be located when he is working with the equipment. This will make the adjustment to the real thing easier.

◇ *Plan for follow-up.* As a part of your one-on-one training, you should come back several times to ensure that the individual is completing the task as you instructed. In particular, you need to look out for shortcuts that may slip into the work and that could lead to quality problems or, worse, raise safety problems. For instance, in one plant, workers found that removing a safety shield on a die cutter increased productivity. It also increased the likelihood of an employee being severely injured.

When Dick explained to his new hire how to use the machine, it never occurred to him to explain why there was a shield in place. So it was very fortunate that he followed up about an hour later. He found that Jim had removed the shield. Worse, it was a suggestion from another worker. The incident became the basis of a group coaching meeting to teach the staff safer operation of the plant's equipment.

◇ *Provide support.* Sometimes a buddy can be assigned to someone learning a new skill, provided you have tested out the employee to be sure that he knows how to complete the task correctly. But in addition to assigning a buddy to an employee you might want to leave the trainee with written instructions to follow. Type the instructions double-spaced or with large margins; give the trainee the sheet during training and allow him to make notes on the margins.

Praising as a Means of Reinforcing Good Performance

Praising is listed separately on the list of coaching duties to indicate its importance as well as to differentiate it from giving feedback. Feedback may be a part of praise, but it also points to those aspects of an employee's work that were not done well, suggesting how future jobs should be handled. Praise, on the other hand, is designed primarily to recognize an employee's outstanding performance and to motivate him or her to repeat such performance.

The problem about praise is that it is very rarely given. Most managers seem more inclined to give criticism than praise. One manager even told me, "I don't have the time to give praise." I know that this manager is extremely busy, but the employee deserved the praise and sought some confirmation that his extra effort was recognized. Because the praise was not forthcoming, to this day that employee goes out of his way to tell others on staff how much he dislikes his boss. Worse, he has gone from being a better-than-average employee to becoming a screwup, which many coworkers believe is an effort to get his supervisor's attention. He seems to be maintaining an internal auditing system and his calculations show that she still owes him one.

When "Praise" Lowers Morale

There is praise and then there is praise. Marta is well aware of the value of praise and would argue that she praises her employees, but she has yet to learn how to use praise effectively. Or, for that matter, what is good praise and what is bad praise. Let me share with you some typical situations in which Marta offered praise to staff members.

For instance, there was the time when Tim, one of her staff

members, completed a research study a few days ahead of schedule. He had worked late several nights to get the report done and ready for her final review before she submitted it to the product manager. As he proudly presented it to Marta, she told him, "I'm so pleased that you completed the report a few days before it is due. Now I'll have some extra time to read it and check to be sure you haven't forgotten to include any critical information."

Tim left wondering why he had put in the extra effort to complete the task ahead of time. Marta had used the occasion only to rub salt into wounds caused by earlier criticism of Tim's past reports.

Or let's take the time that Harry's marketing campaign brought in 10 percent more sales than projected. Marta announced this fact to her staff at its Monday morning action meeting. Everyone was delighted when Marta announced that she had even bought doughnuts and would be providing coffee for all to celebrate the occasion. The staff shared in Harry's success and there were lots of compliments, but the group's enthusiasm quickly waned when Marta casually remarked to a staff member, "Harry's fortunate that he made those numbers. His other campaigns haven't been as successful." She wondered why the party atmosphere suddenly died, but the reason clearly showed on Harry's face.

Marta also will be at a meeting and react enthusiastically to suggestions from staff members. The problem is that her responses are so ambiguous that the group has no clear idea what it is that Marta is so pleased about so that they can work beyond that. I'm talking about comments like, "Interesting remark," "Good," or "OK." Because Marta never elaborates, the puzzled group spends much time talking at these meetings and little time thereafter following through on the "Good" thoughts or "OK" suggestions.

But the worst is the phony praise that often comes from Marta. The staff knows that each day Marta stops by her administrative assistant's desk to compliment the woman on her latest outfit. The phoniness of the daily remark is evident by her intonation and the minimum attention she gives to the woman as she passes her cubicle on the way to her own office.

What, then, is good praise? It is sincere, concise, and specific. And it is delivered in a manner that communicates enthusiasm for the work done or extra effort expended by the employee. For example, "Jim, you really helped us achieve our goal on time by working last weekend." This points up the importance of the employee's activity and, better yet, his contribution to the department's goal or mission.

By inflection or intonation, there is no hidden message in good praise—for example, that Jim should have spent his weekend on the task or that you think that Jim had to work over the weekend because he goofs off most workdays.

As coach, you want your praise to encourage further efforts—in the same way that the climate you create within the department is positive and supports increased performance, or that your feedback is constructive and communicates your faith in the employee's ability to learn a new skills or realize his or her goals or standards, or that you make the appraisal process a means of adding stretch to the goals your employees work to attain.

Your employees are your most appreciable asset. In the next chapter, I am going to show you how you can get that potential we all talk about our employees having but which they so seldom realize.

Chapter 2

Encouraging Stretch

Managers, supervisors, and team leaders know that people are their most appreciable asset. In coaching your employees or team members, your intent is to increase the worth of your organization's human capital. Good coaches are watchers, using their observational skills to determine the gap between employee performance and potential and closing that gap through development of the employee's full capability. After all, you know that as these gaps are closed and your employees fully develop their abilities, they could assume some of your responsibilities, freeing you to work on more visionary projects. In today's lean organizations, managers who don't look for and coach their employees to their fullest capability will have a problem, too.

Compare the coaching performance of Steve with that of Sid.

Coaching From Fear vs. Coaching for Excellence

Plenty of talented employees have worked on Steve's team, but he doesn't really want to coach them beyond their ability to do their current jobs well. Why? He's afraid that if he adds stretch to their jobs, they might in time want his position—and possibly get it. Consequently, all his bright, promising employees have either moved on to greener pastures or are in search of them. When Steve is away on business or vacation or out ill, his crew's productivity suffers because there's no one able to give direction. Steve frequently complains that he has been in the same position for ten years, but actually he is fortunate that he wasn't laid off during the last downsizing. Senior management had wanted to keep only those managers who get high performance from their crews. And Steve is not one of these.

The company's executives want managers like Sid, who is constantly developing his crew members and runs the top crew in the organization. Sid believes that when he has high performance expectations of his employees and communicates these, his crew will work to meet them.

Yes, Sid's department has a problem keeping workers—but for only the best of reasons. As his employees have demonstrated their capability, they have moved on to head up crews of their own or to take on special projects or to assume higher positions within other departments. Does Sid mind? Their departure has caused short-term problems, but he has enjoyed seeing the individuals he has worked to develop into abler and more responsible employees become recognized formally. Besides, as these crew members have grown, so has Sid's worth to the company.

How Sid Encourages Stretch

Sid doesn't just start with good employees. He helps develop his stars by:

◇ Conducting training needs assessments as soon as his employees come on board. He carefully reviews résumés and meets the first day with new hires to identify gaps in information and knowledge, holes that he immediately fills to ensure that newcomers pull their weight as quickly as possible.
◇ Incorporating developmental planning in his quarterly and annual performance appraisals, adding stretch—but stretch within reach of his crew members.
◇ Communicating his belief in his employees' abilities.

Let's see how Sid makes his employees, like Brad, for example, believe they can do much more than they thought they could.

When Brad first came aboard, he seldom spoke at team meetings, lacking confidence in his ideas. It was clear to Sid that Brad had tremendous technical ability but wasn't comfortable speaking in public. Sid worked with Brad from the outset to encourage him to share his insights with the group. He met with Brad privately and discussed Brad's ideas with him, noting how valuable they could be to the group as a whole.

Sid also found opportunities for Brad to demonstrate his creativity to himself so he would feel secure enough to prove it to his coworkers. At first, the pace of discussion during Sid's crew's weekly meetings was too fast for Brad. So Sid slowed the pace enough to give Brad the time to articulate his ideas. Eventually, the group would learn to slow itself down to hear Brad out. Sid also found other teams in the plant in which Brad could make a major contribution but where the pace was slower so that Brad would not be intimidated from speaking out.

With Sid's encouragement and support, Brad's confidence increased until he assumed his fair share of the brainstorming in the department's problem-solving meetings.

As a coach, you can motivate, inspire, and encourage your fast-trackers, but you must also build the confidence of your more timid talents, people like Brad. Your efforts will be repaid time and time again as these individuals use their newly discovered and nurtured talents to become new team superstars.

How to Start

The process actually begins even before one of your employees comes on board, as you sit with potential candidates for a job opening. As you interview the applicants, you will note gaps in knowledge or experience. The individual you ultimately hire may even have skill or knowledge gaps owing to lack of experience in some aspect of the work or unfamiliarity with your own organization's work processes or procedures.

As a coach, your first task in shortening the learning curve for the new staff member, and ultimately building a staff of superstars, is not to get so preoccupied with your own work as to forget the need to fill these learning gaps when your new hire finally arrives.

Besides introducing the new recruit to her coworkers or getting her started on her first assignment, you need to sit down with your new hire to review the job description for the position filled and the concerns you might have about the individual's ability to handle the work.

Your goal is to discuss openly and honestly with her your assessment of training needs. Together, you and your new employee need to develop the first of what will be several development plans during the individual's time in your department.

Bringing New Employees Up to Speed

Some of the individual's deficiencies may be handled by assigning the new worker a buddy; other skill gaps may require enrollment in a training program or a course at a community college; still others may take something as simple as giving the employee your company's procedures manual and asking her to read it carefully. If it is the latter, however, then you will want to meet with the employee after a week or so to ensure that the individual has indeed familiarized herself with all the procedures and understands not only the work procedures but the reasons for them.

Assessing Training Needs

What about employees who are already on staff and perhaps have been with you for some time?

Take a pencil and paper and run through a list of all your employees. Which ones lack some skill that would make the difference between their being a mediocre or average performer and a superperformer? Which ones have potential ability that has not been developed because their current jobs don't call for those strengths? (As you look over your list, you may also identify one or two employees who have performance problems that, in your opinion, require more than training. These persons may need counseling if they are failing to meet job standards because of their attitudes or a personal problem. For help with them, see Section II of the book.)

Once you have identified those staff members who could perform at higher levels with more training, your next step is to meet with each one to discuss your conclusions. Don't wait until the next round of quarterly performance reviews. As quickly as possible, schedule one-on-one meetings with those you believe have the potential to do more. Keep in mind that time lost is productivity lost.

Some employees will welcome the opportunity to discuss their training needs, particularly if they see additional training as a means of increasing their employability. Others will be concerned that your assessment threatens their job security. In discussing your observations with this latter group, you can tell them that the assessment was designed to alert you to the competencies—the skills, abilities, and knowledge—your employees all need. Your intent is not to find fault but to identify opportunities to improve each staff member's performance.

How Training Can Bring Unexpected Benefits

This is how Juan handled Lucy's response to his assessment that she needed to become more adept at using the firm's customer database. During his visits to the work area, he had seen that Lucy often asked Blanche for help in choosing mailing lists for her product mailings. Sales were good, but Juan knew that Lucy was one of his best market managers, as familiar with her product line's customers as the product manager. Consequently, Juan couldn't help but believe that if Lucy had a better working knowledge of the database then sales would be much, much higher.

He wanted her to work with Bruce to learn more about how the database could be used to target product customers. Bruce, a veteran with the firm, had worked with the outside consultant to design the system and consequently knew its ins and outs better than any other marketing manager. Lucy knew how to use the database to market her products well, but she wasn't familiar enough with it to apply her knowledge to another product line.

"Are you telling me that I'm not doing a good job?" Lucy asked in an offended voice, ready to cite capture rates and sales figures in self-defense.

"Not at all," said Juan. "On the contrary, I think you *are* doing a good job. But I think you have knowledge about the market that you aren't applying because you need to know more about how to use our lists. You could do a much better job, and I want to give you that opportunity.''

Presented in these terms, the idea of working with Bruce, one of the best marketers in the company, seemed a compliment to Lucy. So she willingly agreed to call Bruce to discuss getting together for some meetings in which he would share with her his know-how about the system. Juan had already alerted Bruce that he wanted him to train one of the marketing managers.

How did Bruce feel about his new responsibility? Like Lucy, he also saw this as a compliment. After twelve years with the same firm, with a great marketing record but nowhere to go up within the organization, he had begun to wonder if it wasn't time to look for a job elsewhere. Juan's call meant that he recognized Bruce's worth, and that caused Bruce to rethink his future plans. In the end, Bruce never did leave because Juan had other plans for him besides training Lucy on the database.

Enriching Others' Jobs—and Reviewing Your Own

Juan had been asked to take on leadership of several new product teams. But he couldn't take advantage of this opportunity unless he could find ways to reduce his own day-to-day workflow. His solution was to delegate many of his routine tasks to Bruce. Enriching Bruce's job would keep his level of performance as high or higher and also free Juan to bring marketing input into many of the new product efforts that up until then had been exclusively product-driven.

When Juan had called Bruce to alert him to his helping Lucy, Juan had also set up a future meeting with Bruce at which he planned to delegate much of the routine work to Bruce. In time, Juan thought, he could empower Bruce, sharing leadership of the group with him. Maybe even make him into another coach for the team since Juan's intent was to make each of his marketing people superperformers.

Juan began the process of enriching Bruce's job by reviewing his own. He determined which of his tasks he could give Bruce—either delegate or empower him to handle, depending on the nature of the work. As a part of that process, Juan also considered training Bruce might need to assume these new responsibilities.

Should you want to enrich an employee's job and thereby motivate and add stretch to his or her performance, you would need to consider more than training to help the employees you have in mind make good decisions, solve problems on their own, and otherwise work with little or no guidance from you. Your intent in training is to access intellectual capital—in other words, the ability to use knowledge or ideas gained from one experience and transfer them to another.

This is the less formal means of adding stretch through coaching. Let's look now at how performance appraisals can be the basis for developmental plans that can be used to increase your employee's contribution to the company.

The Developmental Side of Performance Appraisals

Each year, after the year-end appraisal, you should be sitting down with each of your employees to discuss strengths and weaknesses. If an employee has encountered problems during the past year, the objectives for the coming year would include some developmental goals. But if you are appraising one of your better workers, then you might want to create goals that add greater stretch than you would ordinarily suggest to your average performers. These goals could be formalized and made a part of the documentation or they could be a part of a wish list that you and your stars agree to work toward but do not include as a part of the evaluation process.

Let's assume, for instance, that you are creating stretch goals for someone like Bruce, an employee who has consistently met or exceeded his supervisor's expectations and is feeling frustrated by the lack of opportunities for promotion or new challenges.

Bruce would welcome goals that represented a challenge and involved increasing his employability through training in skills not for today's work but for tomorrow's opportunities for advancement.

Certainly you would want to make an effort to empower employees like Bruce. Train them in problem solving and critical thinking, familiarize them with the broad picture, and communicate department goals and other critical issues. That should prepare such employees to make good decisions on their jobs.

You might set down on the appraisal form some new standards by which Bruce's work would be measured, like his participation in the department budgeting process or in product management/ marketing meetings or the firm's efforts to expand marketing beyond your country's borders. On the other hand, you and Bruce might agree that you want Bruce to work with you on budgeting for the department, replace you at some product management/ marketing meetings, and become involved in department global marketing efforts, but you might not include these new responsibilities on the form. Rather, you would provide copies for Bruce and yourself, and you would tell Bruce that these were efforts you wanted him to focus on during the upcoming year.

Should he meet his standards for performance as indicated on the appraisal form, as well as realized some or all of the stretch goals, you would acknowledge in the next evaluation his involvement in these efforts and evaluate his performance accordingly.

In developing stretch goals that employees will work toward, you must:

◇ *Involve the employee.* This should be a given, but there are still managers who don't realize that they won't get buy-in to any plan for their employees if they attempt to impose their thinking on them. Even if you make a goal's completion critical to next year's performance evaluation, and achievement of that goal could benefit the employee, you're unlikely to get this person's cooperation if you don't make him or her a part of the planning process.

◇ *Begin at the beginning and go on from there.* The beginning of your task with some top performers may actually be convincing them that they can achieve that goal, as with Tony, who lacked the self-confidence to speak up at team meetings yet was one of the most creative technicians on Carl's crew.

To get employee support for the stretch goals you want to set, together look at opportunities for growth within the department, and determine from the discussion with your stars their interests or aspirations to make the challenges in a re-engineered job more stimulating. If there is a project that the employee can lead, sparing you from this responsibility, discuss it with him or her, pointing to the learning experiences that such an assignment can offer.

◇ *Write down your development plan.* It doesn't matter whether the plan is included on the formal appraisal form or simply written on a piece of paper attached to the form that you keep filed in your desk and review at quarterly reviews and other meetings with the employee.

If your involvement is critical to the achievement of a specific development goal, you need to note that in writing, too.

It's as important for you to assess progress on development goals designed to add stretch to an employee's abilities as it is to review periodically progress on more traditional goals.

Setting Stretch Goals

If you are having a problem with the employee in identifying stretch goals, as a part of the discussion you might ask her, "What can we do to help you maximize your capability?" The purpose of the question is to stretch the employee's self-confidence and get her to begin to think outside the box that is her job description.

You might want to work with the individual to set two operational goals, both of which will utilize the individual's ability beyond what the current job does. Ideally, one such goal might help to create higher productivity, whereas the other might have as its purpose improved operations. To build commitment to achieving the two goals, you will need to focus on why these goals are important by giving factual reasons that reflect business return, not just feel-good reasons. Point to the opportunities and challenges associated with the goal.

As coach, you should make it clear that the stretch goals will likely demand further development on your employees' part. We've talked about the skills your stars will need to learn, but there may also be other skills that they will have to unlearn, and they will need to have patience with themselves and with others as they work to achieve these stretch goals that over time will benefit not only their organization but themselves.

Motivating the Employee

As a part of the exercise, you have to discuss with employees not only why achievement of the goal is important to the organization but also what is in it for them. Here is where good coaches excel. They realize that energizing the workplace through coaching can help energize and motivate employees, but they also know that there is intrinsic motivation that has to do with individual employees' need to achieve their dreams and aspirations. A good coach is able to help people identify these intrinsic motivators and use them to optimize their performance to the benefit of both their organization and their manager.

Questions that can help you unearth these inner motivators include:

◇ What really matters to you?
◇ How can you be more valuable to the organization?
◇ What would make you happy professionally? Personally?
◇ Do you think your professional goals are ambitious enough?
◇ If you had any choice of career or position within the organization, including mine, what would you want?
◇ What accomplishments would build your self-confidence or make you feel better about yourself?

Speak with honesty and listen with empathy so as to better understand how you can support the employee in achieving his or her aspirations. But never make promises.

Making a Goal a Reality

Let's assume that you have been asked to investigate further a new product idea. In your role as coach, you have suggested that one of your staff members take over leadership of the project group in your stead. This individual has an outstanding work record and is a creative thinker but needs to develop more fully her leadership skills. This task will give her on-the-job experience and increase her worth to the organization. So you suggest the idea to her at the time you set outcomes for the upcoming year. She agrees.

This responsibility will truly add stretch to her job. To ensure that she is successful, you meet to do the following things:

1. *Clarify the nature of the task.* In this instance, you and your staff member need to agree that this responsibility represents an area of weakness for her and one of strength for you. But once the staff member masters the skill under your direction, she can take over many of the other projects you might be asked to oversee. You agree that you will meet during the course of the project to ensure she gets the kind of support she will need to be successful in making this stretch.

2. *Identify the goals or outcomes to be reached.* In other words, you clarify expectations. Not only would you describe what you expect of your staff member, but she also could verbalize what her expectations of you are for the life of the project.

3. *Facilitate the task.* In this instance, facilitation is, as defined in *Merriam Webster's Collegiate Dictionary,* "the act of making something easier." Toward that end, you need to listen (think "actively listen") as the employee discusses how she plans to handle the project, and you need to ask hypothetical questions to get her to think about the consequences of some of the steps she plans to take.

Through this process, you may also want to share some of your own experiences even if they are embarrassing. For instance, you might include details about that first project in which you were involved and messed up. Telling your employee what actions worked for you and what actions didn't should be particularly helpful because the stories will minimize the likelihood of this employee goofing up, something that could both discourage her from agreeing to head up another team and seriously reduce her confidence in herself.

4. *Set limitations.* You want the employee to be responsible for this project, but there will be actions that she can take without your approval and others that she will have to discuss with you before proceeding. These are her boundaries.

At this point, you should also discuss the kind of ongoing communication about project progress that you want to receive from the staff member.

5. *Empower the employee.* This step may be the most important action you can take in coaching for increased stretch. It is your agreement that the employee has the right to make decisions and

implement those decisions on her own within the boundaries you both have agreed on.

6. *Backtrack.* Given the importance of the project, you want to be sure that you and your staff member are both in agreement. The best way to do this (think "reality test") is to have the employee state, in her own words, what you both have agreed to. You might say to Claire, "This project is important to our division. I'd like to be sure that we are in agreement about what you will be doing between now and the next time we get together to discuss the project. Could you summarize what we have both committed ourselves to?"

7. *Follow up.* At each subsequent meeting with the employee, follow up to ensure that you haven't forgotten some critical point in your first discussion and that there is nothing that won't be done that should be. If there is some step that is particularly important, you might want to make a note about it, place it in a folder that will maintain all information on the project—from meeting minutes to progress updates from Claire—and put that file somewhere where it is easily accessible for your next meeting with the employee.

Empowerment

Empowering your employees may be one of the most effective ways to add stretch to employees' performance.

The *E* word is gaining currency in management circles as more and more companies demand greater productivity from their leaner organizations. When we empower our employees, we lower decision making to the level of those who report to us. In coaching employees, when we empower them, we demonstrate our trust in their ability to make the right decisions based on the training (think "mind stretch") we have provided. And when they make a mistake, we communicate, by our supportive response, our awareness that even the best employees can goof up on occasion.

Many efforts at empowerment fail because employees are not given the skills, abilities, and knowledge they need to succeed. That's not so likely to occur when empowerment is a part of a coaching effort to boost individual and organizational effectiveness, since training and development are an important element in coaching.

To ensure that you are successful in encouraging employee stretch through empowerment:

◊ *Train your employees for the opportunity.* If you don't, your employees won't be able to handle the work and, equally troublesome, their self-confidence will be eroded, which will make it more difficult to get them to attempt similar stretch in the future.

◊ *Believe in your employees' abilities.* Trust your employees to do the job well. You have to show you have faith in their abilities to make the right decisions. That means being patient when they make the wrong decision.

◊ *Be clear about your expectations.* This is even more important when you empower an employee than when you give him or her a routine task to complete. Your employees won't be successful if they have no clear idea of the results you expect. The results serve as a target by which they can set their course.

◊ *Build on employees' strengths.* In coaching your employees to ensure that this isn't the only time they are empowered, you should focus on those occasions when they do things right. Yes, they will make mistakes and you will need to make note of such incidents. But you don't want these mistakes to discourage your talented employees. In any event, in most instances, the problems can be resolved via training or further coaching.

◊ *Share information.* Put the project, assignment, or task that the employee is being empowered to do within the bigger picture. Without that broader perspective, they aren't likely to make the right decisions.

◊ *Encourage employees to believe in their potential and capabilities.* Help them before problem-solving meetings to see the opportunities there. Get them to look at problems as challenges and to generate creative ideas and to pursue these ideas in an effort to solve the problems.

◊ *Recognize your employees' accomplishments.* If you can't provide financial rewards, look for more challenging assignments to give them further opportunity to demonstrate their abilities. Or, better yet, redesign their jobs to make fuller use of their newly discovered talents and capabilities.

Recognize that not all your employees will be successful in their first efforts at empowerment. As their coach, it is your responsibility to help them to learn from their mistakes—so they can go back and do better the next time. But use your judgment. Some employees lack the aptitude to be empowered. If you suspect after several efforts that this is a problem, give the individual one last chance. If he still isn't successful, then you may want to look at his day-to-day job and identify ways to redesign the job so that it makes the most of his other strengths.

On the other hand, when your top performers are successful, they blaze a trail for their coworkers to follow—a trail that can lead to increased performance throughout the department. In fact, as coach, you may want to make your top talent into assistant coaches, responsible for helping your new and average employees improve their performance.

Departmental Stretch

You build stretch within the entire department by assigning your top performers the task of teaching how they do their jobs well to new and average performers, as Juan did with Bruce. The responsibility itself enriches their jobs. It also brings home to your top talent the important role that their performance is playing in the department. This in itself can stimulate an even greater performance from them.

You can also train your employees to these higher levels of performance by observing how your superstars work and comparing their performance with the behaviors of average workers. By identifying what sets the former apart from the latter, you have the syllabus for a training program that will help those mediocre performers achieve star performance.

Once you know what makes your good performers as good as they are, it is time to begin to hold group meetings in which you share these insights with the entire group. Not only will you increase the level of productivity of the department as a whole but you can also influence the performance of your key personnel as one star learns from another and you, as coach, and your department—as well as your superstars—benefit from the synergy.

Chapter 3

Team Coaching

If you are a team leader, you know that leadership encompasses more than sitting at the head of the group's table. You serve as its coach, and as such you are responsible for:

◇ Ensuring that the group has the right team players.
◇ Creating operating ground rules or guidelines.
◇ Developing a shared sense of purpose in the form of a mission statement.
◇ Translating that mission into goals and objectives.
◇ Enhancing problem solving and brainstorming.
◇ Facilitating teamwork.
◇ Establishing communication channels within the team and outside the team with other groups and operating areas.
◇ Determining the resources needed and providing these or communicating the need for them to the team's mentor or sponsor.

These tasks draw on five critical coaching skills of team leaders:

1. *Setting direction.* The team has to have a clear sense of purpose, and seeing that the group has this depends on the ability of the team leader to clarify the scope, or business purpose, of the team effort. From the first day the group meets through its ongoing progress, the team leader, in his or her coaching role, has to see that the team has a clear sense of course and that it makes course corrections when these are called for. Likewise, the team coach

must see that team members are oriented to the roles they will play within the team structure.

2. *Summarizing.* The leader should summarize others' remarks, not only orally during meetings but in meeting minutes as well. Perhaps even more important, the team leader has to be able to summarize team progress at each milestone and bring together group thinking about the next steps toward achievement of the group's goal.

3. *Facilitating.* The leader must have the ability to maintain an exchange of different viewpoints without allowing dissension to destroy the team spirit that is so important to achieving the final mission. For an effective team, the leader as coach also will be bringing together individuals with different experiences and backgrounds, and thus will need the ability to manage the diversity well without using his leadership position to control the group.

4. *Organizing.* The team leader is the team's administrator, which means that she is accountable for members receiving handouts and agendas ahead of the meetings, receiving minutes within a few days of a meeting, and monitoring completion of work assignments, not to mention assembling a group of individuals who bring the skills the team will need to accomplish its purpose.

5. *Developing.* Finally, you have to teach others the skills they will need to work together as a team.

The importance of these skills becomes more evident as you look at the four coaching roles that you will play during the life of the team: as team visionary, administrator, facilitator, and instructor. You will perform the first two of these roles even before the first meeting of the team and all four throughout the life of a team.

The Team Leader as Visionary

You have to create a group with the potential to be outstanding. That comes, first, from selecting the right people for the team. If there is a team sponsor other than yourself, this is a responsibility you share with him or her; otherwise, you are responsible for bringing the right mix together in order to accomplish the team's purpose.

You shouldn't be concerned only with getting the best people, which means people with the needed skills, knowledge, abilities, and team attitude. The leader should also be concerned with the right head count. You don't want too many participants, since that can slow down team discussion, but you also don't want too few members, since that may cause the team to ignore some key issues. Consider the team's mission in determining the minimum number of appropriate people for the team.

If the team has a narrow purpose, then go for fewer people, and reap the benefits of greater interaction.

If the team's mission will take it into various disciplines in the organization, include representatives from each area, but consider forming subgroups to gain the increased participation and interest that smaller groups offer. These subgroups can report back to the larger group.

If you need a larger group, then your role as facilitator will become more crucial to the team's success. So will the ground rules established by the team.

Setting Ground Rules

Teams need self-discipline, and setting operating ground rules can achieve that. Although the need for ground rules might seem to fall more appropriately under a team leader/coach's administrative responsibilities, they actually belong under his visionary role because the ground rules will affect not only the team process or group interaction but the work to be done. For instance, if the team will need to work with other groups to accomplish its mission, then the need for that kind of collaboration should be indicated in the ground rules with, if possible, the means to achieve it. The following list of sample ground rules should prove helpful.

Sample Team Ground Rules

1. Members will arrive on time and stay for the entire meeting.
2. Meetings will be held every Thursday, from 9:30 to 11:00 A.M.
3. The team will keep to the meeting agenda.

4. A day before the meeting, members will receive a copy of the agenda and handouts to read so that they will come prepared for the discussion.
5. The focus of the team will be on its mission; the group will not be distracted by side issues.
6. The team will allow each member the chance to talk and will hear out other members without interruption.
7. Assignments will be made by the group as a whole.
8. Discussions will be kept to the point and professional; the focus will be on issues, not personalities.
9. The team will meet with leaders of other groups once monthly to review their conclusions.
10. All decisions will be reached by consensus. Disagreements will be resolved by multivoting.

That you are team leader does not mean that you set the ground rules on your own. Rather, you work with your team to create the operating guidelines by which the members will operate; after all, you want the group's members to buy into them. Ground rules established by the team as a whole provide the leader of a cross-functional team without authority over her team members a compelling argument to rethink their team behavior.

To help your team formulate its own ground rules, ask team members to consider what behaviors will detract from the team's mission and what behaviors will contribute to its achievement based on their experience on other teams. This list of questions will also stimulate thinking:

◇ Where and when will meetings be held?
◇ How will emergency meetings be handled?
◇ How long will meetings last?
◇ How will decisions be reached?
◇ How will the team network with others within the organization?
◇ How will the team report to its sponsor or mentor?
◇ How will the team handle conflicts and disagreements among its members?
◇ Will the team evaluate each session after the fact to help improve subsequent sessions?

Ideally, the final rules should be copied for all team members and then hung in the meeting room as a reminder to those in attendance of their commitment to the group.

Creating the Mission Statement

Once the guidelines are set, the team leader takes on a more typical visionary role, leading the group as it prepares a mission statement. Putting the mission in writing—in a sentence or two—ensures that the members have a clear idea of the project's scope (think "business purpose"), the project's time frame, and the group's boundaries (the limits on the members' authority).

To help you write your mission statement, you might want to use a technique called storyboarding, in which the group begins by calling out a few key words or phrases that describe the team's purpose. As team coach, you then work with the group to get an understanding of what individual members mean by the words or phrases, exploring differences and similarities between the concepts, to come up with a final statement of mission.

If the team is finding it hard to complete its mission statement, you can try a more involved approach to storyboarding, in which members list key words or phrases on sheets of paper before they come to the next meeting. Once members arrive, they tape their sheets to a meeting room wall. Now, as team leader, you go through the sheets, circling words or phrases that seem to appear regularly. On a flipchart, write these down and then, as a group, work with the team to fashion the final mission statement.

Don't be concerned if finalizing the mission statement takes more than one meeting. Even though you may have explained the team's objective to each member as you recruited him or her, there may still be confusion about the group's purpose. You want all members to be moving in the same direction. You don't want to have to make course corrections. Having the mission in writing also makes it easier to make those corrections if they do become necessary.

The mission is like a lodestar, there as a guide as you set goals or celebrate achievement of milestones. It ensures that you reach your final destination without unnecessary sidetracks or detours.

Expect some disagreement when you are preparing the mission statement. Len, a production manager from a midwestern plant, told me about a team he led in which one member objected adamantly to the first draft of the mission statement prepared by the team. It was more than wordsmithing. Dave had agreed with the need to streamline purchasing when he was asked by Len to join a group whose purpose was just that. However, at the first meeting, Dave announced that he wanted to narrow the group's focus to concern only raw materials for production. The group's mission, as Len had been given it by the plant's manager, Dean, the team sponsor, was to consider all purchases, from paper to plywood to plastic.

"Dave had complained about all the paperwork he needed to complete just to order #2 pencils," Len recalled. "So his objection to a broader team purpose came as a big surprise. But even more surprising was how vehement he became about the matter." Len soon learned why, however.

The plant is located in a small town, and most of the people there work in the plant. Including Dave's wife, who's responsible for purchasing the plant's office supplies. He had told her about the team's mission, and she had asked him if that would mean lay-offs. "By the time the two of them were through speculating," Len said, "Dave thought our purpose was to install some master computer that would eliminate every job in purchasing, including his wife's."

The first draft of the mission statement was as follows: "We will undertake a study to identify opportunities to reduce paper-work and eliminate duplicate work processes in purchasing and complete that study, with recommendations for change, by June." After Dave's objections, the group came up with this alternative mission statement: "We will undertake a study to identify opportunities to better utilize existing staff in purchasing and complete that study, with recommendations for change, by June."

Dave still wasn't totally happy, according to Len, but he said he could live with that mission. Which means that the group had reached its first consensus decision.

The Team Coach as Administrator

Most management books don't say much about the administrative tasks of a team leader as they relate to his coaching responsibility.

But as the team's coach, you are responsible for guiding and, to some extent, controlling the discussion. You can do this in part by ensuring that meetings begin and end on time and overseeing preparation of the agenda, distribution of handouts, and even preparation of the meetings' minutes.

Team leaders themselves should write the minutes of each session rather than assign the task either to an administrative assistant or another team member. By retaining the responsibility to put in writing the conclusions reached at each session, you ensure that the minutes reflect the scope initially set for the group. Poorly written minutes can actually sidetrack a team.

In writing the minutes, you may also see evidence that the team is losing its direction. If so, you will need to address this issue at the next meeting.

Mastering the Administrative Details

Let's look in greater depth at your administrative responsibilities as a coach.

As with your role as visionary, they begin before the first team meeting takes place. You will want to arrange for a room to be set aside for your team during its lifetime. Having your own meeting room will allow you to put on the wall not only the team's mission statement and operating rules but also charts of team mission milestones and member assignments and their status. If you can't get a meeting room, see if you can set aside a part of the employee lounge for regular meetings after work hours; graphs then will be visible for all staff to see, further motivating members of your team.

Members will also have a hideaway from their day-to-day workstations in which to complete their team assignments on time. And members will interact outside the team meetings, which should build better rapport among the whole group. Informal chats can stimulate brainstorming that will carry over into the meetings.

You will also want to arrange the furniture in the room in a way that best encourages the exchange of information and ideas. This is called proxemics, using room setup to encourage team dynamics. For instance, if you want to maintain maximum control of the meeting, you would set it up like a typical classroom, with you in front of the group. But if you want more participation and greater interaction among team members, you should opt for a table, either a round table, if you want to minimize your role as team leader/coach, or a rectangular table, if you want to maintain your leadership role with a little help from proxemics.

The first meeting's agenda should include time for setting ground rules and finalizing the mission. If the team's sponsor is to be present, that should be indicated on the agenda as well. Don't just list the actions you want to accomplish during the meeting; also specify the amount of time you estimate each activity will take. And include the means by which the activity will be accomplished. For instance, if the team's sponsor is going to begin the meeting with a welcome, indicate that he or she will be addressing the group. Note that development of the team mission statement will involve a group discussion, as will the setting of ground rules. Whenever possible, be as specific as you can be.

You should set the agenda for the first meeting. But thereafter, you will want input from members of the team. If you have a corporate intranet, you can set up a file in which members can make additions to the agenda up to two days prior to the meeting.

Meeting agendas and any related materials should be distributed to members at least two days before the meeting to give members an opportunity to study the handouts. If you have a corporate intranet, you can put this information on the network in a file dedicated to the team rather than on paper. You might even want to create a file in which copies of all documents related to the project will be kept so that those on the team can replace lost reports or other materials distributed during the life of the team project. This file would also contain copies of all minutes.

In putting together your minutes, here are some tips:

1. *Offer an overview in the first paragraph.* Write a compelling lead sentence to draw readers' attention to the minutes' contents. Don't waste the first sentence with information about the date and time of the session (place that information on the subject line). Focus on the key conclusion, like, "The marketing task force was held to review competitive information on five firms. Of interest to the group, in particular, was these firms' ability to increase

market share by distributing their product line in smaller communities. The team agreed to study the obstacles to our firm's doing the same."

2. *Organize meeting activities into information shared, discussions that took place, and decisions made.* Use boldface headings for each major category and italics for subsidiary information to make it easier for the minutes to be scanned by team members and others (like the team sponsor or mentor) with whom the minutes are shared.

3. *Make clear what the follow-up issues are.* If some issues came out of the discussion that weren't addressed but that the team believes need to be followed up, you may want to include the category "Pending Issues" as well.

4. *Don't go into lots of detail.* Just give the reader the facts. You should focus on the key points of a discussion and the important decisions that were reached and their implications. It's not necessary to review everything that was said. While someone had some nice things to say about the packaging proposed for the group's new product, that information doesn't belong. In the minutes, however, should be a summary of the competitive study done by Marcy and Alex.

5. *Remind members of the assignments that came out of the meeting.* Besides mentioning the dates of upcoming meetings, you want to remind team members of their commitments for the next session. If the discussion led to a number of tasks being delegated, these assignments should be noted, along with due dates for each and the name of the team member responsible for the work.

6. *List the names of attendees at the end of the minutes.* You should indicate who was at the session, but you want to focus members' attention first on the substance of the minutes.

With the minutes, you may want to distribute a first draft of the agenda for the next meeting. This will prompt members to make their additions then and there and return the document to you. If you've sent the minutes via e-mail or used the intranet to share the minutes with the group, you may need to send an e-mail message to remind team members to add their ideas to the e-mail message or agenda on file on the network.

One final bit of advice about your administrative responsibilities: To ensure punctuality and good meeting attendance, ask team members to bring their calendars with them to the first meeting. Set aside a regular day and time for meetings and have members note these times on their calendars through the planned life of the team. This makes it easier for members to make each meeting.

The Team Coach as Facilitator

When managers and team leaders are asked to list a leader's coaching responsibilities, facilitation usually heads the list. And understandably so. As facilitator, the team coach is responsible for helping to make the discussion run smoothly, occasionally identifying and remedying team behavior that impedes the team's performance.

As facilitator, you should communicate to members that all ideas are welcome. Clarify poorly worded ideas for the group. When someone gets off the track, you should prevent discussion of the irrelevant issues without discouraging the member who made the remarks.

Your goal is to get participation from all, which means encouraging quieter members to talk while discouraging domination by others. All this is done subtly during the meeting itself. (Facilitating problems that aren't so easily remedied is better handled after the meeting, in a counseling session, as discussed in Chapter 7.)

Incidentally, if you can share this facilitation role with team members, providing team members with facilitation training prior to start-up, you will take some of the pressure off yourself for ensuring an open communication climate. The group as a whole may work together to create a positive, collaborative environment for problem discussion and resolution.

The following case study provides some insights into how a team coach handles his multiple roles to guide the team past its internal obstacles and toward its goal.

COACHING A TEAM PAST OBSTACLES

Joe, a marketing VP, found himself leading a high-visibility team for a consumer products company. His company had undergone numerous problems during a twelve-month period—from a series of downsizings to a product liability lawsuit that it lost. Concerned about the effect on sales, the firm's directors had asked management to form an image-building team to assess the impact of these events on customers' perceptions about the company and to determine what damage control to attempt.

Management wanted all product lines represented on the team, so eight people—marketing and product managers—were asked to meet every Thursday from noon to 2:00 P.M. to undo the damage to the firm's image over the last twelve months. They were an articulate group, but they also had very decided views about their product lines, the events' impact on sales, and action steps to recommend. Jeb Thomas, the CEO, didn't make Joe's task any easier.

Jeb had been asked by the board to be there for the first meeting, ostensibly to make clear how important their purpose was. But in the course of his remarks, it became clear that he was truly a "doubting Thomas" about the need for the team. If the past events had created some problems with the corporation's image, they were short-lived; he thought that in the interim the firm had regained its rosy image in the eyes of its customers.

After he left the room, no one said a word. Finally, Barbara spoke up, "If Jeb is right, what are we doing here?"

"Worse," Carole said, "if he's wrong—and I think he is—how do we present that fact to him, let alone submit suggestions to address the problem?"

Joe then spoke up. "Whatever Jeb thinks or doesn't think," he said, "should not interfere with our mission. Let's get down to work. We'll start with setting some ground rules."

The Importance of Ground Rules

That Joe and the team set the ground rules prior to working on the group's mission statement made it easier for him to coach the group through creation of the two-sentence objective; even then it took two weeks of heated discussions. "Barbara was the worst breaker of the rules throughout the life of the team," Joe recalled. "Whenever we discussed any subject related to her product line, she would get defensive. She would interrupt the speaker by jumping on his words, then take control of the discussion. On several occasions I had to retake control of the team from Barbara and refocus the discussion on the subject of the previous speaker," Joe told me.

Carole represented another kind of problem. Usually so outspoken, she was silent during many of the discussions "She was uncomfortable confronting the political issue involved—Jeb Thomas's lack of support for the team's mission," Joe observed. He found he had to ask her very specific questions to get her to participate in the group. Dwayne, on the other hand, was very outspoken, and Joe found that he had to wait until the product manager paused for breath, then ask for another member's opinion on the issue.

"Maria, a marketing manager, wasn't like Barbara or Carole or Dwayne," Joe continued. "Whereas the rest of the team, despite the political ramifications, wanted to do a good job, Maria just wanted to get the whole thing over with. We would be barely into a subject, when she would call for a vote, insisting that any further discussion was unnecessary." Joe would then ask Maria to state the issue on which she wanted a vote. He would next ask team members if they agreed with her conclusion that they had reached the point of making a decision or whether more discussion was called for.

The team had numerous heated discussions, but Joe was able to facilitate the discussion, and ultimately the group came up with a six-step program to submit to the board that included a customer-focused campaign in local newspapers in target areas where image problems existed.

Ten Strategies for Successful Meetings

During the course of the team meetings, Joe utilized ten strategies that he said helped him get through a tough six months. He would:

1. *Ask for feelings or opinions.* Except for Carole, Joe didn't have a problem drawing people out, but he did find that asking questions like the following encouraged further discussion: "What brings you to conclude . . . ?" (which demanded that Barbara verbalize many emotional responses to what was being said); "What prompts your suggestion to . . . ?" (which got Maria to verbalize

some of her reasons for calling for a vote); and "What are some other ways you think we could . . . ?" (which enabled others besides Dwayne to speak).

2. *Paraphrase what others had said.* By asking one angry member to repeat in her own words what another member had said that caused the anger, Joe found that he could prevent arguments from breaking out. He too would paraphrase others to ensure clarification for the group as a whole: "Let me see if I understand your position. Are you suggesting that . . . ?" "What I am hearing is. . . . Am I right?" "Let me restate the last point you made to see if I understand."

3. *Call on the quieter members for their reactions to comments on more vocal members.* Besides Carole, Joe used this technique on Darlene, Ted, and Erik: "Darlene, how do you feel about what Dwayne just said?" "Erik, how would you answer Maria's question?" "Before we move to the next subject on the agenda, I would like to hear from Ted on this issue. What are your thoughts on the issue?"

4. *Ask for a summary.* Periodically Joe would stop the discussion to review what had been covered so far and any decisions reached. Not only did this keep the group on course; it also allowed the group as a whole to catch its breath after a heated discussion: "Before we go on, can someone summarize the points we have made?" "I have heard a number of ideas from the group. Would someone summarize what has been agreed upon?" "It is evident that Barbara disagrees with what has been said. Barbara, could you give us three reasons why?"

5. *Ask for more concrete examples.* This moved the discussion from the abstract to the specific, from information to actions that the team could propose to improve the firm's image. "Erik, can you expand on what you just said? Could you give me some examples of what you think we could do?" "Are there other things we should consider?" "Maria, since Ted handles your product line, could you add to what he said?"

6. *Question whether the group had reached consensus.* Since Maria seemed to want to move on before the rest of the group, Joe found he often had to ask: "Maria believes Erik's suggestion should be a part of our recommendations. Does everyone agree?" "Dar-

lene, do you agree with Maria that we have fully addressed this issue?" "Maria believes that we can go on. Let me see a show of hands if you all agree."

7. *Call for action.* Joe would ask, "How do you think we should proceed?" Or, more specifically, "Dwayne, how would you suggest we proceed?" Or, looking to the group as a whole, "I'd like your suggestions on possible ways we can get started researching. . . ."

8. *Suggest the next step.* "Since we never get to some agenda items, should we rank in priority the items on our agenda for next week?" "Barbara obviously has some very strong views on this topic. I suggest we go around the table and see how the rest of the group feels." Joe even used questions to get the group to take a fifteen-minute break during the two-hour session: "Who would like to take a break?"

9. *Support a team member.* Joe found that supportive statements like the following helped get members of the team to share their feelings: "Barbara, you've had your chance to share your opinion. Let's hear from Carole now." "Let's give Darlene a chance to describe her experience." "Dwayne, you've had your say. Now it's Ted's turn."

10. *Confront disagreements.* "Carole, you haven't said anything, but I suspect you disagree with what Ted just said. How do you feel about his comments?" "Barbara, I get the impression that you aren't satisfied with my explanation. Is that right?" "Maria, is there something here you disagree with?"

In short, Joe found that he could stimulate discussion by asking the group a general question and that he could cut off discussion by asking the group to summarize the discussion to date; that he could bring a quiet participant into the discussion by asking that person a general question; that he could get the attention of two participants involved in a side conversation by asking one of the two parties a specific question; and that he could get an assessment of the group's progress on a topic or on a debate between two outspoken members of the team by asking for a member of the team to summarize what had been said.

Finally, at the end of the project, Joe asked the team one last question: "How well did I do as team leader?"

He got high marks from his team.

Critical Thinking

As manager, you should see that staff members who lack them are instructed in the skills and abilities they need to do their jobs well. Likewise, as a team leader, you or someone with whom you contract should instruct your team in skills like problem solving and decision making, even facilitation, since it will make group dynamics a lot easier for you as the group's leader.

Right now, most organizations still reward teams as a whole rather than individual members on the basis of their personal contributions to the endeavor. But for those of you who work in an environment in which team members will be asked to evaluate each other's efforts, then you will also have to coach team members through the assessment process.

The most important skill for any problem-solving team is critical thinking, which is accomplished through a distinct, eight-step process that should not be confused with traditional problem solving. The following table, which lists both processes side by side for convenient comparison, reveals the uniqueness of critical thinking despite a few obvious similarities with the traditional process.

Traditional Problem-Solving Process	Critical-Thinking Process
1. Definition of the problem	1. Definition of the problem.
2. Diagnosis of the cause	2. Collection of all information relevant to the problem
3. Development of alternative solutions	3. Identification of as many possible causes of the problem as you can think of
4. Evaluation of alternative solutions	4. Selection of the most likely cause
5. Selection of the best solution	5. Use of creative problem-solving techniques to brainstorm as many solutions for removing this cause as possible
6. Implementation	6. Evaluation of the solutions based on factors critical to success

7. Selection of the best solution based on these factors
8. Creation of a plan of action to implement the chosen solution

The eight-step critical-thinking approach to problem solving avoids some of the problems associated with traditional problem solving:

1. *Not clearly defining the problem.* Most problems aren't in neatly wrapped boxes. Before a team can solve the problem, it needs to be certain of the exact nature of the problem.

2. *Making assumptions about the cause of the problem without facts or foundation.* If a team is to define a problem, it has to know all the facts and to be sure of what are facts and what are merely assumptions. Too often, teams attempt to resolve problems on the basis of long-held assumptions, gut feelings, and guesswork, only to find that the problem recurs because such assumptions proved false.

3. *Lacking a structured approach to solving a problem.* Teams often don't use a structured approach to problem solving, although even the simplest of problems can benefit from the mental discipline of the six-step problem-solving process or, better yet, the eight-step critical-thinking approach that combines creative thought and analytical ability.

4. *Stopping with the first good idea.* It's as if team members hear a clock in the background ticking. So they look for a quick fix rather than extending the brainstorming to identify three or four good ideas from which they can choose the best. Maybe this is a reflection of the fact that we all seem to be spending too much time on teams.

5. *Making snap judgments.* Often teams will discount any ideas with flaws in them rather than isolate their best elements and try to build on that, or attempt to bring together the best of several ideas to create a superbest idea.

You will also need to teach your team the specific techniques it can use to verify assumptions about the cause of a problem, from

Pareto Analysis to Scatter Diagrams, to Workflow Diagrams, to Cause-and-Effect Diagrams, and you will want to teach your team creativity techniques like free association (which includes brainstorming) and forced association (which uses metaphors and analogies to generate ideas).

You will also want to plan implementation of your team's solution. If team members have not had any experience in this, this is another area for instruction. So, too, will consensus decision making be if you have decided to use that approach to come to final decisions. Among the subjects that you will have to instruct the team in is multivoting, in which the group slowly reduces the number of choices by vote.

Each time the group votes, the list is reduced by half. In time, a list of, say, fifty good ideas can easily be reduced to a workable number for further study and final decision making.

If you have only a few ideas, you can call for a vote to determine if you have consensus on one. Keep in mind that consensus doesn't mean unanimous agreement on one idea but rather choosing an idea that everyone can live with.

What if you can't reach consensus after considerable discussion? Make the decision yourself, after listening to opposing opinions. This may be your toughest job as team leader, in the role of coach. But then that's why professional coaches get all the big bucks, right?

Chapter 4

Coaching Traps and Problems

Well done, coaching can boost individual and organizational effectiveness. Poorly done, it can alienate employees and undermine performance. Let's look at the most frequent traps coaches fall into and how to avoid them.

Hiring the Wrong People

Professional coaches hire the best. Managerial coaches should do likewise, yet too often managers/coaches settle for less.

Many coaches wait until they have someone on board before they worry about job performance rather than begin the coaching process even before someone is hired in order to make sure that they get the very best person for the job. Sloppy hiring procedures may leave a coach with a problem performer, somebody he might never have hired if he had known then what he now knows about the individual.

Often, all it takes to identify people with the potential to do good to outstanding work is to hold lengthier interviews, ask more targeted questions to learn about job skills and attitudes, and schedule follow-up interviews either with you or, better yet, with other interviewers. Multiple interviewers generally increase the range of questions as well as provide a variety of perspectives for consideration of applicants. Barbara may find out some things about the applicant that Casey didn't, but Casey may learn some things that Barbara didn't. And Doreen may discover some interesting things about the candidate that neither Casey nor Barbara did. *Case in point:*

THE RIGHT OUTCOME FOR TWO MR. WRONGS

Two managers had interviewed a young man for an opening in the accounting department; the two managers would have to share the employee because they had budget enough only for one new hire, although there was sufficient work for two assistants.

This young man was favored over another man, Brad, who was less articulate but brought to the job similar experience and skills. Both Thérèse and Mark still weren't sure; although they both liked Norman, there seemed something wrong, so they asked Fannie to meet with him and Brad to get a third opinion.

Fannie spent an hour with each of the applicants, then met with her colleagues to share her opinion. She agreed that Norman was extremely articulate, but she pointed to something that neither of her peers had noticed in meeting with him: He had never held a job for more than a year over a seven-year period. When questioned by Fannie, he had offered numerous explanations for leaving the jobs; in one instance, he admitted that he had been fired. He explained that he disliked high-pressure situations and he had been fired when he was insubordinate to his boss. Fannie admitted that Norman made a great first impression, but, as she sarcastically added, he should. "He has had lots of practice interviewing for jobs." And, she added, "I don't know if he will stick around here. He has unrealistic expectations about how quickly he can move up in an organization. When he discovers that he can't be CEO after a month with the company, he will likely get wanderlust again."

Brad didn't fare any better. Fannie had asked him questions designed to get some sense of his flexibility, which is critical when one is working for two managers. "Brad has a better job record than Norman," Fannie said, "but I think he would have a hard time in the kind of unstructured work situation the job you have entails."

Fannie suggested that the two managers pass on both candidates and take a little longer on their search. Mark was willing to try to make do with Brad, working around his deficiencies, but Fannie made a good point: "The best way to prevent having to spend considerable coaching time with an employee, let alone deal with a problem employee, which could occur with Brad, is to select someone with every reason for succeeding on the job." To do otherwise would ensure that both of her colleagues had headaches down the road.

Allowing Disorientation to Continue

Coaches who neglect to orient an employee or postpone orientation may find themselves with a potentially effective employee whose work is starting to flounder. Such employees are off track because no one has taken the time to put them on the right track by clarifying the performance level expected of them or filling skill gaps first identified during recruitment but neglected in the hurry to get them to work.

Aware of a new hire's shortcomings during interviewing, we often plan to close that gap with training—either off-site or on-the-job—once the individual is at work. Unfortunately, by the time this person arrives on board, the situation has gotten to the point that our first thought is to get him to work. We don't undertake a training needs assessment or develop a training plan for the individual to ensure that his performance is up to standard, let alone review with the employee the job description and discuss specifically our expectations for his performance.

Employees shouldn't be forced to fill the gaps in either expectations or skills by trial and error. The likelihood is too great that they will make mistakes, injure their self-confidence, get reputations as poor performers, and become subjects not for coaching but for counseling.

Making Implied Promises

Many managers make the mistake in coaching of suggesting that added effort on an employee's part could land her a promotion or a high rating and big raise. It's unwise to use such a promise as an incentive unless you can truly deliver on it. A broken promise can undo any improvements in the performance of the employee as well as cause you to lose your credibility with both your staff and the employee, who will tell all how she was fooled by you.

Sometimes, when coaching, in order to leave an employee with no misunderstanding, you may even have to raise the issue just to squash it. That is what Neil had to do with Jenny.

He wanted Jenny, a bright and talented new hire, to take a course in marketing for nonmarketing personnel. As head of marketing, Neil had found that it always helped if his assistant had an appreciation of the discipline and an understanding of the jargon. But Jenny saw much more in his request. She had told him during her interview that she wanted to move into marketing, and she believed that Neil had decided to put her on a fast track to marketing assistant. Fortunately, however, Neil became aware of her wishful thinking. He didn't discourage Jenny from pursuing her career goal, but he did disabuse her of the belief that a promotion to marketing assistant would directly follow completion of the course.

Changing Management Styles When Coaching Doesn't Work

Good managers, like good coaches, practice situational management, adapting the degree of direction they provide employees to their experience and self-confidence and to the nature and importance of the task assigned. But there are some general guidelines in coaching that remain pretty much the same regardless of employee or circumstance: the need for open, honest communications; mutual respect; recognition for excellence and outstanding performance; and shared responsibility for decisions and implementation. These aspects of coaching aren't things you put on when it is convenient but discard and replace with more autocratic overwear when things don't go as smoothly as the textbooks suggest. If you do that, you will find it difficult, if not impossible, to re-establish the positive relationship that you had as coach. Trust between you and your staff goes out the window.

What could cause you to lose faith in coaching as a managerial approach to employee performance?

Let's assume that you've been put on the spot. Plant management is installing new production equipment, and it wants your crew to install the equipment and be prepared to go on-stream with it in a month, six weeks at maximum. You tell management that you can't get it done in that time period unless it allows for overtime and extra staff during the transition. Management agrees. Now you have to tell your staff.

You have spent considerable time building rapport with your staff. You know that the changeover will come as a surprise to them, but you believe that your crew members trust you enough to know that you wouldn't commit them to such a tight deadline unless it was imperative to their continued employment or unless you believed that the deadline was feasible. Both of which were the case in this instance.

So you are more than shocked when the employees you have nurtured, trained, and empowered oppose the plan. Rather than calmly discuss the reasons for your staff's resistance, and make an effort either to convert your employees to your course of action or achieve some compromise, you tell them that they have no choice; you even threaten retribution if they don't work hard, including putting in overtime, to make that deadline.

THE COACH WHO LOST HIS COOL

Hal, a manager in a southwestern electronics plant, found himself in just such a situation. Hal felt that he and his staff had reached a higher level of communication and that his employees would acquiesce in any request he made of them. So their opposition to his announcement that the staff had one month to install and go on-stream with new production equipment left him annoyed. The greater the opposition, the more he lost control of his temper.

"How could you commit us to something like this?" Doris asked stridently. "We need at least two months to master use of the equipment." Doris was informal leader in the group, and after she spoke the doubt among crew members developed into outright opposition. Hal found that his efforts to tell the group how it would be possible to implement the plan were drowned out by vociferous team-member resistance.

Rather than try to restore order and discuss his plan coolly, he raised his voice and angrily told the employees to shut up. "You have no choice," he told the group. "The equipment will be installed in March. You will have it on-stream by April 1."

"Sure," Doris said, "April Fools' Day. Which is exactly what Hal is if he thinks we will do what he wants."

Hal overheard. Later in the day, he had words with Doris about her attitude, which only further solidified opposition to the plan. There was talk in the department about going over Hal's head to discuss the plan with the plant's manager.

Hal's Basic Mistakes

Changes in an organization never come easily, and this was a major one at the plant. Hal wrongly assumed that his time spent as coach made it unnecessary to consider how best to tell his team about the change, which as a manager, faced with a major operational change, he should have done. Coaching is not a panacea, a cure-all that will make all management situations you encounter a breeze. But Hal's bigger mistake was to revert to a dictatorial manner when his group questioned his judgment. He violated some key responsibilities of a coach, from listening to staff members' opinions to involving them in the decision and its implementation.

While Hal had made a commitment to senior management, after explaining to his staff the reasons for having done so, he could have asked the group for its ideas about how the changeover might be handled in the tight time frame given them.

As a manager as well as coach, Hal should have thought through the announcement. As with getting support for any changeover, he should have considered the kind of opposition he might run into and should have tried to build support even before the announcement. From his coaching, he knew his employees well and he could have used this knowledge to predict each member's reaction to the news. He should certainly have talked to Doris, who, as informal team leader, could have helped him get buy-in to the plan. As coach, he could have made her project leader; since the position represented a growth opportunity, Doris would then have had more reason to give vocal support to the plan. At the very least, a conversation with Doris would have clued Hal into the kinds of responses he could expect. This would have allowed him to anticipate what to say in response to the resistance. He could even have practiced his responses before the staff meeting to ensure a calm reaction to the employees.

In this instance, he could have told his team why the equipment changeover was so important to the plant. Once his employees understood its importance to their work and, more germane, the capacity of the plant and consequently its continued operation, their attitudes very likely would have changed dramatically. He should also have considered what answers to give to questions that the group might have had, for example:

◇ What steps would be taken to acquaint the crew with the new equipment?
◇ What would be done during the interim to ensure that work on the old system continued until the changeover?
◇ What team rewards, if any, would be associated with a successful changeover? Even recognition by plant management would have been a persuasive factor in building support for the idea.

Hal got the changeover completed in a month, but it took him a lot more time to repair the rift in his relationship with his crew that his angry reaction to its response had created.

And One More Mistake

Hal hadn't considered how his crew would respond, and he lost his cool, but he also made another mistake. He began to talk *at* them, not to them, about the change. He said, "I want this done," and "I expect you to make it a reality," and "I promised you would do it, and you will do it." He even went so far as to practice a little fear management, implying that failure to achieve the transition in the time allotted might force management to make some reassignments of crew members in order to place on the crew those who would be quicker learners.

Instead of this heavy-handed response, Hal could have shifted pronouns and adjectives from *I* and *you* to *we* or *our,* thereby reinforcing the sense of team that likely would have made even the one-month deadline less threatening to the crew.

Undermining Employees' Self-Esteem

I have mentioned the importance of the pronouns you use. The same is true of adverbs. When giving feedback, beware of correcting behavior using words like *always* or *never,* or other adverbs that could undermine a worker's self-esteem, suggesting that he or she *never* does anything well. For instance, you shouldn't say, "You are always late," or "You never complete work on deadline," or "You try all the time to get out of work." Instead, be specific. "Marie, on September 4, you were late by a half hour. What was the problem?" Or, "Michael, while you were traveling on business, I expected you to call. Why didn't we hear from you?"

Focusing on Attitudes

Just as feedback that makes use of exaggerated adverbs isn't constructive (think, instead, "destructive"), so too is judgmental attitudinal feedback. Suggesting that someone is lazy or argumentative or uninterested in her work is demoralizing, more likely to decrease the individual's level of performance than otherwise. After all, attitudinal feedback gives employees little direction to help them improve performance; it suggests no specific actions they can take to do so. Besides, such feedback is not legally defensible if it shows up on the employee's evaluation and is used to make a decision about a raise, a promotion, or, worst of all, continued employment.

Rather than tell an employee that she is "lazy," better feedback might be, "You don't lend a hand to other workers and, instead, have been frequently seen reading a novel or the newspaper, although your coworkers would welcome your help." Rather than tell an employee that you think he has no interest in advancement, you might note how he has turned down several training opportunities or refused to participate in some high-visibility projects. Or if a customer service rep is short-tempered, particularly when customers ask lots of questions, rather than accuse her of being argumentative, you might tell her, "Mildred, customers complain that it is very hard to get product information from you. As a result, some customers have confided that they are going to competitors."

Failing to Follow Up

Some feedback is better than no feedback. Managers who don't assess their employees beyond the quarterly or trimester appraisal reviews aren't giving their employees sufficient information to help them increase their performance. But feedback is as important, maybe more so, when you delegate an assignment to an employee or when you train one of your staff to master a new skill and even more important when you empower him or her to do something. Feedback at these crucial junctures may make it unnecessary for you to give negative feedback at the quarterly reviews or end-of-year evaluation.

THE IMPACT OF FOLLOW-UP FAILURE

The product line for which Sophie, a marketing manager, was responsible had had a tough year. Part of the problem was that the home improvement tools she marketed had been on the market so long that there didn't seem much more that she could do to interest potential buyers. Consequently, when she and the product manager came up with the idea to market the tools in grocery stores to housewives who had small repairs to do, Sophie looked forward to the planning meeting at which she would present the idea to senior management, including the potential sales figures.

Busy number crunching for the meeting, Sophie asked Irma to use the demographics she had developed to prepare graphics to go with her presentation, which would be on Monday at 10:00 A.M. Because the presentation was a full week away, Irma, Sophie's assistant, had plenty of time to do the work.

In the interim, Sophie was busy with numerous chores herself, in and out of meetings and knee-deep in paperwork for what was called by marketing managers "hell week" (or "planning," as senior management called it). Sophie didn't think to ask Irma about her progress on the graphics. She had hoped to check with her on Friday afternoon, but a last-minute meeting with sales distracted her.

Need I tell you what happened on Monday? First thing that morning, Sophie went to Irma and asked her for the graphics. Irma looked at her and said, "I forgot." She pointed to the stacks of paper all around her workstation as explanation, became upset as she saw the grim look on Sophie's face, and began to cry. Sophie just stared at her. Without the graphics, she would have a much harder time getting the money she would need to position the product line in a whole new marketplace.

Who was to blame? Sophie, of course. Why? As Irma's coach and supervisor, she didn't do what she should have done: follow up.

Even before that, she should have clarified priorities when she gave Irma the assignment. By making clear that this wasn't just another clerical assignment, Sophie could have minimized the chance of such a situation happening. If Sophie had told Irma that the graphics were crucial to her presentation, it is possible that Irma, aware of their importance, would have put aside all the rest of her work to do the best job she could on the graphics. At the time, all Irma knew was that Sophie needed some graphics prepared on the basis of a bunch of numbers she had given her; there was no reason to suspect that the job was more important than the correspondence and other tasks she had to do.

But Sophie could have ensured that the work was done on time by following up during the week to see what progress had been made on the assignment. She could even have told Irma that she would need to see black and white proofs by Wednesday. By Thursday, she would want to look at the color proofs with any revisions. "By Friday," she could have said, "the final charts should be done."

Follow-up is equally important when training an employee in a new skill or procedure. Once you have shown the employee how to do the task, then had him explain the steps in the task in his own words, then asked him to do the work to show you his comprehension of it, and left the employee with some written instructions to remind him about each step, you have only taken the first steps in ensuring that this employee performs the new skill correctly.

You haven't finished with training unless you come back about an hour later to see if the employee is doing the work as you instructed. If he isn't, then you point to those steps in the process he is doing correctly before noting the mistakes he is making. Otherwise, you will destroy the individual's self-confidence in his ability to learn how to do the task. Then you and the employee go through the training process once again: You do the task, ask the employee to explain how the job is done, then watch the employee as he does the task correctly.

Done? Not quite. You should visit later in the day—say, a few hours later—to check again to see if the work is being done correctly. At the end of the day, you might also stop by to see about the employee's progress with the work. If all looks well, you can tell the employee so and recognize his accomplishment. If there are still problems, you should discuss calmly and quietly the nature of the problem.

Let's assume that all is well. Done? Not yet. Stop by the following week to be sure that all the steps in the process are being followed as they should be. If it is imperative that each step be done as instructed, then you want to make that point clear to the employee and make sure that he hasn't developed some shortcuts that erode the quality of the final work.

If there continues to be a problem, you want to discover why.

Placing the Blame

The first response of most of us when an employee is having trouble completing a single task or performing the job as a whole is to assume that this person knows the nature of the problem and is capable of solving it. Often this isn't the case. Further, when we hold this view, we can build up resentment toward the employee whom we begin to think is just doing the work wrong to make us look bad or to get out of a task or to get even for some slight.

It is usually better to begin with the assumption that the communications on our part were somehow inadequate. We didn't make clear how important the work is, how this work is to be done, or how important this work is in relation to the other tasks to be done. Repetition of the instructions may help to clarify the cause of the problem.

Let's get back to the employee who doesn't seem to be learning how to complete a task and whom we have instructed twice about the work. If the employee is to do the task correctly, we have to find out the cause of her confusion. If English is a second language, that may be behind the problem. If she lacks some basic information essential to doing the task, then you should go through these fundamentals before going over the steps in the task again. Another source of problems can be the employee's own desire to do more; she may have introduced shortcuts in the process to impress us, but these may actually undermine the quality or quantity of the work. In plants, as we have seen, such good intentions on the part of new workers can even create conditions that make accidents more likely.

Ignoring the Problem

We've got so much work to do and so little time in which to get it done that it's easy to take the course of least resistance and become blind to staff shortcuts or other less-than-perfect efforts. Unfortunately, when we ignore these small problems, they can grow to the point that they are no longer coaching problems but are now issues for counseling.

A "Small" Problem That Mushroomed

Lynn, head of systems, had come up with the idea for a monthly department report that would be distributed to department heads and other senior managers in the company. The report's purpose was to ensure financial and management support by making these individuals familiar with past accomplishments and future opportunities through use of the new technology. Copy was provided by systems engineers and users and given to Roxanne, Lynn's assistant, who was responsible for producing the final pages using in-house desktop equipment. The report was printed off-site.

The latest issue came out, and as Lynn quickly looked through its pages, she noticed lots of typographical errors. Roxanne was responsible not only for keyboarding the content and logistics but also for editing and proofreading the report. Lynn had seen a few errors in the past, but she hadn't talked to Roxanne about them; she knew that Roxanne had been busy assisting in the development of some technological updates and follow-up training, and Lynn didn't want to come down on her after such a hard week. Besides, Lynn had to admit to herself, she had enough on her own plate; she didn't have the time to deal with something like a few typos in the "constituency" report. But their number had continued to increase. Lynn knew that she had to talk to Roxanne about the situation. Very likely she would have postponed her conversation once again if she hadn't overheard a conversation between Roxanne and another assistant, Marilyn.

Marilyn had noticed the typos, too, and had asked Roxanne if she wanted another pair of eyes to help proofread the report. "No," Roxanne replied. "It really doesn't matter. Most readers won't notice."

As Lynn listened, she was appalled. "Of course, it matters," Lynn thought to herself. "This report went to senior management, and its purpose was to send a message to top management about the department's commitment to excellence—*in everything*." She called Roxanne into her office.

"Roxanne," Lynn began, "I looked over the report. There are some really great items in this month's issue, but I also noticed several typographical errors. I like to issue this report because it reflects the very best work done by the team. These typos, small as they are, diminish that image."

"Oh, come on," Roxanne said. "They aren't that noticeable. If they were, I would have stayed late to fix them before I sent the pages to the printer. But we've had errors before and no one has said a word. Even you," Roxanne finished.

"I noticed before," Lynn admitted. "I should have spoken to you about them earlier," she continued. "Would it help if we asked several of the other assistants in the department to read copy, too?" she asked, moving the conversation from a criticism of the work to development of an action plan to prevent the problem's recurrence.

Was Lynn to blame for the few errors growing into many more? Yes. Like Sophie, who didn't make clear to Irma the importance of having the graphics in time for a presentation she was making to senior management, Lynn had not made clear to Roxanne how important it was to produce a "perfect report" for distribution to senior management. By her failure to say anything, Lynn had given Roxanne the impression that she could get away with not always doing her very best. But it was the last time she let any member of her team think so.

Not Recognizing Improvement

Acknowledging good performance doesn't have to mean big dollars. Recognition for a positive change in behavior can come in the form of praise and other positive reinforcements. Unless you acknowledge performance improvements, no matter how small they may be, however, these small improvements aren't likely to be permanent. Nor are they likely to be followed by bigger improvements over time.

Your time commitment to getting people motivated and keeping them motivated doesn't have to be much. About ten to twenty minutes in a meeting with staff each week, on Friday afternoons, to review what the group has accomplished should be sufficient. Such a meeting would allow you not only to celebrate staff accomplishments but also to acknowledge what individual members of the team have done—to name these staff members and be specific about their accomplishments so all can join with you in recognizing them.

Failing to Give Direction

Too often, you know your department's mission or goals, but you fail to share them with your staff. Or you might tell your employees the department's goals but then fail to keep them informed of progress toward those goals. Either kind of inaction can diminish employee motivation.

Without information on department goals, your staff won't have a focus. And without any indication that they are closing in on the short-term goals and overtime can accomplish the long-term goals, they will grow weary.

When you share your group's goals with members or, better yet, when you set them with your team as a group, you should also discuss the bigger picture—how the department's goals align with corporate goals. And at that point you also want to discuss with the group how you can keep team goals in front of members daily, like hanging progress charts that are updated daily or having a department newsletter (like Lynn's) or Monday morning meetings with coffee and Danish courtesy of the company.

Being Impatient

Finally, coaches can easily fall into the trap of losing their patience after having explained the same task for the tenth time, learning about a stupid mistake that will cause a project setback, or reading a simple memo that needs editing.

Coaches who fail to exhibit patience in such circumstances are sending a message to their employees that they "can't believe just how stupid they are." Patience sends a very different message; it tells employees that the coach recognizes that they are human beings and, as such, they have human fallibility, yet that is no reason to quit. Rather, as human beings with the capability of developing and improving their performance, employees understand their boss's patience as evidence that he or she believes that they can succeed in their work. So they should *try again.*

Section II
COUNSELING

Chapter 5

Switching to a Counseling Mode

Based on your coaching, you can boost both individual and department or division performance. But that hard work can be undone by just one staff member who doesn't carry his weight. Work output may be poor or below standard. Due dates may be missed, affecting the work of others down the line. The employee may lack initiative and seem uninterested in the job, behaving as if every workday was a blue Monday. Or he may be continually late or absent, *by coincidence*, almost every Friday.

Managers know that they are responsible for intervening in the event of such problem behavior, particularly when that performance affects others' work within the department or the work of the group as a whole. But too often managers don't act—despite such costs as:

◇ *Lost productivity.* A poor performer produces only about one-third the work of average workers.

◇ *Lost business.* Problem performers aren't likely to extend themselves to get or keep an account or to handle difficult customers tactfully.

◇ *Lost time.* Poor performers take up a disproportionate amount of supervisory time, as much as 50 percent. This means that there isn't much time left for the rest of the staff, including time to coach them.

◇ *Lost talent.* Many of your best workers, as they lose respect for you and begin to doubt the fairness of your evaluations, will job hunt; your less productive workers will stay, but, no longer afraid of you, they may try to get away with the same stuff as your troublesome employees.

◇ *Lost self-esteem—yours.* As you firefight to make up for shortfalls in the problem performer's work, you may become angry and frustrated and burnt out. In time, you may lose your self-confidence. This could affect your own job performance—and others' perception of you.

Failure to Take Action

Given these consequences, you have to wonder why managers don't take action before a performance problem escalates to these levels. Numerous explanations are given, from overidentification with the employee's feelings, to lack of faith in the human resources department to support the manager's actions, to reluctance to play judge and jury over another's career. Let's look here at three key reasons why:

Fear

Managers worry that they will lose control of the discussion as the employee cries or gets angry, that the effort will end in the employee being fired, and that ultimately they will find themselves in court defending their actions. Such fear is understandable. Articles in the press citing six-figure awards to plaintiffs in lawsuits about unfair discharge are more than enough to scare a manager with a problem performer, particularly if that individual is a member of a protected work group. It's a lot easier to engage in wishful thinking that the performance problem will resolve itself; either the problem will disappear or the employee will leave on his or her own. But neither happens very often.

If it helps you as a manager to confront a long-term employee about a performance problem, and counsel her to turn her work around, think of what you must do as a version of Tough Love—"tough-love supervision."

Tough Love is a nationwide program designed to aid troubled teens and their parents. It's a program that encourages young people to take responsibility for their behavior. And three of Tough Love's ground rules can be adapted to counseling:

◇ Its goal is to remedy poor performance, not to demean a person. Annoyance is directed at the work and not at the employee.

◇ It is based on a genuine desire to see the individual do better. If you keep this positive attitude in mind, you won't feel as if you are destroying another person's career by bringing up her performance faults. You are actually helping the individual.

◇ It seeks to achieve agreement with the problem performer and together build an action plan to turn the employee's performance around.

Crisis Management

Another reason why performance problems aren't addressed has to do with today's leaner organizations. With so much to do and so little time in which to get it done, managers can become so accustomed to crisis management that they aren't as aware as they might otherwise be of everything happening around them. Problems that they should notice go unnoticed—until someone or some incident brings it starkly to their attention. Even then, however, they may do nothing. They make the mistake of not doing anything because they see counseling as too time-intensive. They think it is easier to fill the performance gap themselves, although, given their schedules and the importance of their organization's strategic intent, it is a terrible waste of their time to do the undone work of one of their employees.

Lack of Training

Although training in counseling skills would enable a manager to resolve individual performance problems that diminish the productivity of the entire department, few companies give new supervisors or managers or team leaders the instruction they need to help them with troubling or troubled employees. This is unfortunate because counseling is a responsibility and, like most managerial responsibilities, can be mastered with training and experience.

Counseling Defined

The semantics associated with counseling may actually be more complex than the process itself. Some define counseling as an ongoing process for development, and they define coaching as a means of addressing specific performance problems. There are others who consider counseling as one element of coaching (they also throw mentoring into the coaching pot, too).

Does it really matter what we call one process or the other? Not really. But it is important that you be clear about the purpose of each process as you use it.

When we talk about counseling, we are referring to a nonpunitive disciplinary process, the most important step of which is one-on-one meetings with the problem employee in which your purpose is to get the employee to acknowledge the difference between actual performance and expected performance; identify the source of the problem; and develop an action plan to bring performance at least up to minimum expectations, if not higher. The secret to good counseling is in the communication process, and that entails the following three practices:

1. *Communicate openly, directly, and honestly.* Don't be ambivalent about telling an employee that he isn't doing the job that you want done. If you hem and haw about a performance problem, talking around the topic rather than being clear about its nature and seriousness, you leave the employee with the mistaken notion that you aren't really concerned about the situation, and that there is no need to change his behavior. At the least you leave the employee confused, at worst you leave yourself open later to a lawsuit based on your failure to make absolutely clear to the employee the problem with his performance and the implications of a continuation of that behavior.

You need to make clear that you're talking not only about the effect on work itself and the standards by which the individual's performance is being measured—your expectations of the employee—but also the consequences of continuing poor performance, like being denied a raise or, worse, the start of progressive disciplinary action, which ends in termination if the problem continues.

2. *Practice active listening.* In particular, you want to learn how to use silence to encourage the employee to talk about what is happening in the workplace, the problems she is having, and what she will do to achieve the results you want.

Certainly, you don't want to dominate the conversation, lecturing the individual about her performance problems. Rather, you want to create a dialogue in which you speak only about one-fifth of the time, thereby practicing the 20/80 rule. Setting a conversational tone also minimizes the likelihood of the discussion turning into a confrontation while increasing the likelihood that you and the problem employee, together, will come up with a workable action plan for turning her performance around.

3. *Probe and question.* The key to one-on-one counseling is, first, to ask open-ended questions that will identify possible causes of the problem performance, then to ask more pointed questions to determine the specific cause. You can then follow up with a closed-ended question to confirm your conclusion: "Although you say you have a clear idea of your responsibilities, isn't it true that you have a hard time prioritizing your assignments?"

If you consider these three skills, it should be evident why all three are so important to counseling: They enable you to make clear to a problem performer that she is accountable for a certain level of performance, that you are not receiving that level of performance, and that you expect that improvement. When you practice all three at once, you create a supportive environment in which a problem performer feels free to open up to you and discuss what is behind her misbehavior or performance deficiencies. Then, together, without demoralizing the employee, you can both define areas for improvement and agree on an action plan for achieving that improvement.

If your communication style already is a combination of assertiveness, active listening, and probing, then you are fortunate. But if you aren't there yet, don't worry. Developing a counseling

style is something that can easily be learned. Listening and probing skills come with practice; and assertiveness comes with self-
confidence, with practice, and with documentation that supports
your comments about the employee's performance.

The Need for Counseling

If you are fortunate, you won't have to apply your counseling skills
frequently. After all, many shortfalls in performance can be handled during the performance appraisal process, at one of the three
or four meetings you hold during the year.

   If you've planned your appraisal reviews correctly, you've set
aside an hour or more for each of your employees and therefore
have sufficient time not only to identify their accomplishments but
also to discuss failures in their performance and create action plans
to ensure that they will reach the standards for their job or meet
their goals by the end of the year.

   Generally in appraisal interviews you will be discussing situations like an employee's failure to follow up with a vendor on an
order (an oversight), a staff member's reluctance to utilize fully the
new office technology (need for additional training), or an employee's failure to complete a market research report on schedule (work
overload, need for a temp). Unless these problems are a part of a
pattern, they usually can be remedied through some coaching in
the form of training or direction.

   Performance problems that will demand counseling include
continuing poor work quality or quantity, frequently missed deadlines, disorganization, chronic tardiness or absenteeism, frequent
and lengthy disappearances from the workstation, lack of initiative
or even a total lack of interest, with the employee seemingly wish-
ing to be anywhere other than at work, lack of cooperation, and
even insubordination.

   Some of these problems will be found to stem from skill deficiencies, others from repetitive or unstimulating jobs, still others
from post-downsizing depression or grief, or burnout, or frustration about being asked to do the impossible without the equipment, funds, or time to get the assignment done, a condition in
many of today's downsized companies. Other performance prob-

lems, like making disparaging remarks about the company, the boss, or work to others within and, worse, outside the organization, like customers, or refusal to follow instructions, or minimum output but maximum complaints about department policies or procedures, or sulkiness or uncooperativeness, may stem from an attitude problem rooted in a conflict with you, a peer, or corporate policies or procedures.

Finally, many performance problems can be traced to personal problems in the employee's life, from financial difficulties to divorce, to a chronically ill child or parent, to an emotional problem, to substance abuse. A study by the National Institute on Drug Abuse found that substance abusers are late three times more often than the average worker, sixteen times more likely to be absent, four times more likely to have workplace accidents, and three times more likely to use health care benefits.

Let's look at a situation in which there was a need for counseling, but the manager was unaware of it until it was brought to his attention—by staff, peers, and his boss through a 360-degree feedback program.

How 360-Degree Feedback Opened Charlie's Eyes

Charlie is the manager of an office supplies warehouse on the East Coast. In an organization that had severely downsized the year before, he was so busy fighting fires that he was blind to the existence of a problem others saw, a situation not unique in today's fast-paced companies.

Charlie got the first inklings of a problem after his company instituted a 360-degree feedback program in which managers get feedback from various individuals—from their boss to their staff members to peers to customers. His boss, staff members, and even some peers gave him low marks for developing his employees.

A 360-degree feedback program has various purposes. At Charlie's company, it was designed for developmental purposes. Consequently, managers were encouraged to go to those who gave them feedback to get a better understanding of the conclusions and create self-improvement plans to increase their management skills.

When Charlie met with some of his peers, he found them reluctant to explain why he had received such poor ratings as someone who helped to train and develop his workers. Charlie felt that he had done a "pretty good job": Two of his employees had even been chosen by these very peers for jobs in their departments.

Depressed by the loud silence with which his query had been greeted, he asked his best friend, Pete, why he had gotten 2s and 3s, on a scale of 1 (worst) to 5 (outstanding), from his managerial buddies.

Summing Up Gloria

Pete wasn't so reticent with Charlie: "It's Gloria," he said. "Everyone else in the plant is working himself or herself to death, yet Gloria sits outside your office and reads romance books or the newspaper in the morning, runs around spreading rumors, refuses to help others because she says she's too 'busy,' and complains about the organization to anyone who will listen, from colleagues to customers, yet we all know that you haven't done anything about it. You probably don't know what's happening because you keep your door closed all day."

Charlie didn't know how to answer. He kept his door closed because the noise outside his small office made it hard to concentrate otherwise. But each time he stepped out and saw Gloria, she seemed very busy.

"Gloria has worked for me for ten years," he explained. "She has her peculiarities, but I can count on her when the chips are down," he answered.

"I don't know," Pete replied. "You asked, and I told you."

As Charlie drove away from the office that night, he thought about Pete's comments. Clearly, Pete wasn't aware of Gloria's strengths. Yes, he concluded, Pete was wrong. He'd ask his staff members the next day what they thought of his assistant to prove that Pete was mistaken.

Reinforcing Pete's Assessment

Which is what Charlie did. When Gloria went to lunch, he brought Michael, Richard, Joe, and Barbara into his office and asked them about the 360-degree feedback they had given him. They all had nice things to say about Charlie until it came to the question of developing employees.

"We all think you are great," said Barbara. "Yeah," Michael agreed. "Sure," said Richard. Joe, a longtime member of Charlie's department, didn't speak.

"Okay, Joe," Charlie said. "I've never known you to be speechless. So what's wrong?"

At first Joe denied any problem, but under Charlie's prompting Joe finally told him, "It's Gloria, Charlie. I've known Gloria as long as you have, but her attitude bothers me. And your failure to notice it bothers me even more."

When Charlie looked at the faces of his other staff members, he could see that they were in agreement.

At that point, he had to leave his crew to meet with his own boss about his evaluation. Ed had been Charlie's boss for less than a year, and the two had often come to blows initially as Ed, a tough task-oriented manager, adjusted to Charlie's more people-oriented work style.

Charlie expected lots of feedback from Ed, but actually Ed had only one complaint. Yes, you guessed it—Gloria. It seemed that Gloria had been rude on the phone to one of the firm's biggest clients. "I know that it's important to you to be liked by your people," Ed said, "and I might not be as concerned about how my people feel about me so long as I know I have their respect. But I can't understand your support for Gloria. There have been some meetings in which she has spoken out in a very disrespectful manner toward you. How can you put up with her?"

"I spoke to her . . . ," Charlie started to say, then stopped. It suddenly occurred to him that he had spoken many times to Gloria about her behavior and attitude, and over the short term there had been improvements. And then the problems began again. Because he had worked with her so long, knew her husband and kids, and even went to ball games with the family in the summer, he no longer had an objective eye on the problem.

Asking the Tough, Self-Analytical Questions

It was time for Charlie to ask himself some tough questions about Gloria (*questions that you should be asking about the members of your staff*):

◇ *Am I making allowances?* In Charlie's case, it was true that
Gloria knew how he operated and often anticipated his needs, but
it also was true that she had to be told to do some things more
than once, refused to take on new responsibilities as the department
became more electronic and the work had to be given to other secretaries as overtime, and would testily let him and anyone else who
called Monday mornings know that she wasn't happy to have to
work for a living.

◇ *Do I feel angry?* As Charlie watched Gloria slip away from
her desk to gossip with the new temp, although she knew he needed
the report she was retyping by 3:00 p.m., had several pages to go,
and it was already 2:30 p.m., he had to admit that he was angry. If
the report was to be done on time, he would have to take some of
the pages and type them himself.

"It wasn't the first time," Charlie thought. Suddenly he realized
that he was being taken advantage of. "No wonder I go home frustrated because I haven't done as much as I could—I'm doing some
of Gloria's work," he realized.

◇ *Have I used my own busy schedule as an excuse to avoid
confronting the problem?* While Charlie certainly didn't deliberately
use his workload as an excuse not to sit down with Gloria and discuss some incident or other when she was out of line or didn't perform as she should, he had postponed meeting with her time and
time again. He would tell himself that he would bring up the matter
during the next appraisal review, but at the review he would either
touch only lightly on the matter or ignore it in his rush to complete
the review.

◇ *Am I acting more like a father or mother or a personal counselor than a boss?* Relationship-oriented managers like Charlie estab-
lish a rapport with employees that is part of what makes them
effective. However, in a close relationship, employees may share
personal problems with a manager that sometimes encourage the
manager to offer personal advice that could aggravate the personal
dilemma. In these circumstances, it is better that the individual see a
professional counselor (think "psychologist," "psychiatrist," "family
counselor," or "financial counselor") who can help the employee
get to the true nature of his dilemma. The manager may listen and
express concern, but he shouldn't let the circumstances inhibit him

from his primary responsibility: improving the employee's performance at work.

As he considered his behavior with Gloria, Charlie had to admit that his chats with Gloria had made him aware that her husband, Jerry, was having work problems, and this had most likely made him go a little easier on her than he would otherwise have done. He certainly had said nothing about her frequent phone calls to Jerry or her long conversations on the phone. Like a father, he had gruffly reminded her of the costs, but he hadn't said anything about their effect on Gloria's productivity or the ability of customers to get through to the sales department or, most important, her work performance as a whole.

◇ *Are staff members angry or jealous?* Charlie didn't have to think hard about this question. While Joe alone had spoken up, and then only after some prodding from Charlie, Charlie knew that Michael, Richard, and Barbara, as well as Joe, were annoyed. Over lunch, they probably asked each other, "How come good old Charlie lets Gloria goof off but runs us ragged?"

◇ *Is the situation becoming the topic of conversation?* Unfortunately, Charlie didn't have to think too hard to answer this question, either. It was yes. His 360-degree rating made that evident. If he didn't correct Gloria's performance, he would be judged poorly not only by his staff members but by his peers as well. Even his boss had grown tired of hearing Charlie defend Gloria.

Once Charlie accepted the existence of a problem, his next step was to visit with Human Resources to discuss what he would have to do to turn around Gloria's performance.

Understanding Counseling

When we think about counseling, we usually think of the one-on-one meetings with employees regarding their performance shortcomings. Actually, counseling involves more than that. Counseling is a process, and that process is a part of most corporate performance management efforts.

Most organizations have two counseling tracks: one for performance problems, another for rule violations and other misconduct. The existence of two tracks reflects the fact that rule violations are a more serious issue than a shortcoming in job performance; besides, poor job performance is not necessarily a deliberate act of the employee and can often be corrected with either training or positive reinforcement.

Since the purpose of this book is to help you boost the performance of your employees, counseling for improving job performance and increasing individual and organizational effectiveness is the focus of this section of the book. Before we continue with that discussion, however, let's take a brief look at the procedure companies often use for handling rule violations or other misconduct.

Counseling Misconduct Cases

Counseling for rule violations or other misconduct differs from performance counseling in that it begins immediately with a verbal warning. This is followed by a written warning if the violation or other offense is repeated. Depending on the nature of the offense, the employee may be suspended without pay for a specific period to rethink his behavior. A repetition of the rule violation thereafter is followed immediately by termination.

Specifically, as the following list indicates, disciplinary counseling is at most a five-step process. The actual number of steps depends on the seriousness of the conduct, the work history of the employee, and how the employee responds to the initial steps, or warnings.

The Five-Step Disciplinary Process

Step 1. Issue a verbal warning. The verbal warning is usually used when the misconduct is minor or it is the employee's first offense. It lets the employee know that you are aware of what he has done and that you expect him not to repeat the offense.

Step 2. Issue a written warning. If the verbal warning isn't heeded and the employee repeats the violation, or if the offense demands more than a verbal warning but not a reprimand, then you might want to issue a written warning in memo form. A copy is given to the employee and one is placed in his or her personnel file.

Step 3. Reprimand the employee. Often this reprimand won't be given by you but rather by your own boss or someone in your firm's human resources department. The message here is clear: Another repeat of the incident, and the employee will be suspended or terminated, depending on the nature of the offense.

Step 4. Suspend the employee. This action is taken in the event of repeated misconduct or a serious offense. Sometimes the employee is paid while he is away from work, sometimes he is not—the nature of the situation often determines that. The employee is expected to use the time away from work to do some soul searching about his desire to stay with the firm and, as an integral part of that, his future conduct.

Step 5. Terminate the employee. If the problem still continues, then the employee is terminated. Generally no thought is given to a demotion since the assumption is that the employee is at fault, as opposed to the case of a poor performer who has tried to turn his or her job performance around but can't quite do it. Depending on the misconduct, termination may actually be the first step and not the last step in disciplining a problem performer, for instance, in cases like extreme violation of safety rules or theft.

The Four-Step Performance Counseling Process

Performance-improvement counseling involves four steps: verbal counseling, a written warning, demotion or transfer, and termination.

Step 1. Verbal Counseling

Most often, counseling takes the form of sit-down meetings with employees over a period of time, but it can also take the form of a simple, spontaneous remark to an employee, such as, "Hope, you should be at your desk now, shouldn't you?" or "Sam, I thought we agreed that you would have that report on my desk by noon?" Frequent informal remarks can also signal the need for a sit-down meeting.

Both informal and formal counseling should be documented. That notation would include your observation and remark and the date and time of the incident. There is no question that documentation is critical not only in counseling but in any efforts to boost employee performance. In the case of counseling, your notations can suggest the beginnings of a pattern of poor performance. Reviewed prior to an appraisal meeting, they may even enable you to avoid counseling entirely by nipping a potential problem before it blossoms.

If you need to counsel an employee, you are better positioned, with the documentation you have kept, to prove to the employee that there is, indeed, a problem despite the employee's arguments to the contrary. And arguments you will hear can range from "I used to be that way but I've recently improved," to "You don't understand how hard I have to work," to my favorite, "You are right about my strengths but totally wrong about these problems."

Step 2. A Written Warning

Most corporate progressive discipline programs demand that employees be issued a warning before they are moved to more severe discipline, like a demotion or termination, if the counseling sessions aren't working. The warning is usually presented in a written memo. Upon its receipt by the employee, you and he would meet again to review the employee's plans to improve his performance. This meeting with the employee would be documented and, along with a copy of the warning, the description of the meeting would be placed in the employee's personnel file. At this point, it should be made as clear as possible to the troubled or troubling employee that a continuation of the problem could mean his separation from the company.

Step 3. Demotion or Transfer

A demotion or transfer is not a cop-out in instances in which the employee's performance isn't his or her fault and, for whatever reason, training or extra direction from you will have no effect. A case in point:

HANDLING A NON–TEAM PLAYER

Mitch was hired as a marketing researcher before his department reorganized into teams. Over time, it became evident that Mitch wasn't a team player and was much more productive working on his own than in a group setting. He would try but invariably he would become frustrated by the time spent as a part of the product group, go off by himself, and complete the team's project on his own. His efforts were excellent, but frequently their implementation went poorly because of a lack of buy-in from the team's members, who resented being left out of the problem solving.

Mitch was fortunate because his boss was able to transfer him to a position, at his current salary and level, in which Mitch could work pretty much alone, analyzing others' research on prospective joint ventures before consideration by senior management.

But often transferring an employee who doesn't perform as required is not a viable option for his boss. If, for example, an opportunity for a transfer to another job or another department doesn't exist, then a manager may have no option but to demote the employee or to terminate him.

Where the situation allows for a decrease in the person's responsibilities and subsequent lowering of his grade level and pay, then you may want to demote the staff member rather than terminate him if corporate policy gives you such an option. Even though a lower grade can be demoralizing to the individual over the short term, it is better than being terminated. Termination is really your only other option because retaining an employee despite his failure to fully do the job is unfair to those other staff members with the same job who must meet the higher standards for the work.

Step 4. Termination

The numerous wrongful termination lawsuits and multimillion-dollar judgments may worry you so much that you would rather tolerate poor performance than fire the staff member, but one of your responsibilities as a manager is to identify employees who are not working up to standard and correct their performance shortcomings. If an employee continues to make repeated mistakes or fails to satisfy department goals or standards, or to act as if he or she would prefer to work elsewhere, then you are justified in letting that individual go.

Keeping on the employee will only create further management headaches for you, as the efficiency and effectiveness of the group as a whole are pulled down by the poor performance or attitude of the unrepentant subperformer.

In terminating the employee, just be sure that you have documented your attempts to turn the employee's performance around. It will also help you if you stay in touch with Human Resources during the counseling process to ensure that you don't fall into any legal pitfalls (see Chapter 8).

Preparing for a Counseling Interview

Let's return now to Charlie, whom we left as he was on his way to the human resources department to discuss his problems with Gloria.

CHARLIE SETS UP A COUNSELING INTERVIEW

After meeting with Human Resources to understand better the firm's policies and procedures for counseling a poor performer, Charlie called Gloria into his office to discuss with her the client's complaint about her and other problems with her performance. He didn't blame the need to counsel her on his boss or anyone else. He was up-front with her, taking responsibility not only for his failure to act sooner but also for the decision to meet with her to develop an action plan to overcome whatever performance problems existed. She was resistant but agreed to discuss the matter further with him. So he scheduled a counseling interview with her. And thus Charlie began the counseling process with Gloria.

Counseling worked with Gloria, for those who would like to know. But, as Charlie admitted, it wasn't easy.

Contrary to the impression that management textbooks seem to give, counseling interviews aren't a cinch. These one-on-one meetings have five goals, which are listed below (and reiterated and expanded in Chapter 6, where they form the core of the chapter), and they aren't successful unless all five are achieved.

1. Win the employee's agreement that there is a need for change.
2. Identify the cause of the problem.
3. Agree on the specific actions that the employee will take to improve his or her performance.
4. Follow up regularly with the employee to ensure that she is reaching the goals you both have set.
5. Recognize the employee's accomplishments to reinforce continued correct behavior.

During your interviews, there is a sixth issue that you should address as well. It isn't frequently mentioned, but it is important. You must make a determination as to whether the effort is really worth it. Not only should you consider the problem employee's track record with your company, her motivation and willingness to change, and worth to the organization (the talents she could bring to the department if the employee worked to standard or beyond), but also the worth of your time spent counseling the individual.

If the problem with the employee is so deeply rooted that you honestly doubt you will succeed, or if counseling will demand more effort than you have the time to give and you know you are unlikely to follow through to see if the employee does make an effort to turn around her performance, then it may be better to consider your two other options before investing too much time in one-on-one counseling: either transferring the employee to another area within your organization where this person can perform more effectively, or terminating her.

At the very least, you may want to shorten the amount of time you give to counseling—from, say, two months to one month. And if there is no improvement, then you may terminate the individual. Most companies don't specify the amount of counseling required before a warning is issued or the employee is terminated. The option is usually yours, although you should discuss the person's background and any actions you would like to take with Human Resources to be sure that you are on safe legal grounds (in particular, have the documentation to justify your decision).

Think of it this way: You don't want to spend so much time on a lost cause that you won't have counseling time to give to other subperformers with greater potential for improvement or, for that matter, enough coaching time to provide to those average employees who could become outstanding performers. Furthermore, you don't want to distract yourself from projects that are of bottom-line importance to the department.

When Counseling Fails

When Len took over the circulation department of a major magazine publisher, he found that he had inherited a major performance problem in the person of a forty-nine-year-old, ten-year veteran with the department: Phyllis. He also had to reorganize the department to handle work associated with the firm's decision to publish a major new magazine. Len had to ask himself if he could turn Phyllis's performance around after two other managers had failed to do so and still give the restructuring all the attention it would need to ensure good customer service to the magazine's charter subscribers.

Corporate historians reported that a problem with Phyllis's performance had been evident after she had been with the company only six months. Her then-supervisor, Bert, had done little about her missed deadlines, poor paperwork, and other work shortcomings. Bert "didn't like to make waves," which meant, among other things, that everyone in the department got the same rating, a 3, meaning that all met standard—which Phyllis's performance certainly did not.

After five years with the company, Bert moved on to another job in another company. After working with Phyllis for a few weeks, Bert's successor, Todd, decided to do something about her performance. Keeping careful documentation of her performance, he was able to demonstrate to Phyllis that she did not deserve a rating higher than a 2. That was the rating Todd gave her the first year the two worked together.

A Short-Lived Success

Phyllis promised Todd that she would improve, and together they set intermediate standards as a first step toward Phyllis's performing at the same level as everyone else in the department. The effort seemed to work. In six months, Phyllis had met the intermediate standards. Renewal mailings went out on schedule. Invoices didn't have errors on them. Phyllis came in bright and eager each morning and stayed until after 5:00 p.m. to be sure that the paperwork was in order. When the firm had a special supplement to mail, Phyllis even worked through lunch for several weeks to help, something previously unheard of.

Todd was pleased with Phyllis's performance. While her performance wasn't at the same level as that of her co-workers, the change in her attitude was so dramatic that Todd decided to give her a 4 to continue to motivate her the second year the two worked together.

Resuming Old, Bad Habits

Immediately thereafter, though, Phyllis's performance began to decline. She always had an excuse, but Todd knew the truth: Phyllis had slipped back into her old habits. He was about to begin counseling again, and was even considering putting Phyllis on warning, when he was offered a new position in the magazine's New York office. Before Todd left, he had an opportunity to talk to Woody, his replacement; Woody promised to put an end to her cavalier attitude toward her work while the rest of the department worked itself to exhaustion. And Woody did try—at first.

He began meeting with Phyllis once every two weeks to check on her work, and once again she responded positively. But as the department's workload increased, Woody had less time for Phyllis. Once again, this led to a decline in her performance.

Another Managerial Compromise

Woody recognized what was happening. As long as someone kept at her, Phyllis would do the work as she should. But if you turned your back for even a few days, her performance declined.

Woody knew that he should begin the counseling process with the intent of terminating her if there was no significant, long-term improvement, but he felt that he didn't have sufficient time to hold the counseling sessions, document the meetings, issue the warning memo, and so forth. He worried about Phyllis going to court over a decision to terminate her after she had been with the company seven years and had received 3's and even a 4 most of that time.

In the end, Woody chose to give Phyllis a 2 each year, which, according to the firm's appraisal program, meant that she "met some standards but not all." Since a 2 still meant a raise, albeit a very small one, Phyllis did virtually nothing in the three years before Len replaced Woody as head of the department.

When Len looked at Woody's evaluations, he couldn't understand why Phyllis hadn't been terminated sooner. He knew the department would be assuming even more work in the near future, and everyone would have to pull his weight to get the work done. Phyllis would drag down the entire group's effectiveness and efficiency, and Len decided to act immediately.

Len Lowers the Boom

With the support of Human Resources, he met with Phyllis and told her that the department's role in the company's expansion made it imperative that everyone do his or her full share. He placed her on warning, which was justifiable on the basis of past appraisals submitted by Woody. No one in the department was allowed to perform at a 2 and stay, he said. Phyllis had one month to meet the work standards by which her peers were measured. Further, if her performance declined at any point thereafter, she would be terminated immediately.

This happened two months later. She had tried to play the same game with Len that she had played with Todd and Woody, but Len wouldn't have it. He knew that he would have had to keep meeting indefinitely with Phyllis to get a full day's work from her. And he didn't have the time. No manager with a problem performer has that kind of time.

After reviewing Phyllis's history with the company, Len had answered the question all managers must ask themselves before they begin counseling a problem performer: Is it worth the effort? In Phyllis's case, the answer was no.

What about any problem performers on your staff? Keep in mind that time is a very important asset today, as important as your best performers. You can't become such a nurturing manager that you fail your first responsibility: to get the job done.

Chapter 6

The Counseling Interview

There are five objectives that you will need to accomplish when counseling problem performers:

1. Win the employee's agreement that there is a need for a performance change.
2. Identify the cause of the problem.
3. Agree on the specific actions that the employee will take to improve his or her performance.
4. Follow up regularly with the employee to ensure that he is reaching the goals you both have set.
5. Recognize the employee's accomplishments so as to reinforce continued correct behavior.

These five goals are important whether you are counseling an employee with a work-related problem or one with a personal problem that is influencing job performance.

Let's look at how each of these goals can be achieved.

Goal 1: Win Agreement

To put the problem employee at ease at the start of the meeting, you can open the session with a variant of the following: "Jennifer, there's something that's concerning me and I need to talk to you about it," or "Michael, there's something bothering me and I need to see if I can get your help in getting it taken care of." Once you have the employee's attention, you can then move on to the nature of the employee's problem behavior by describing what was expected of her and how she is failing to meet that expectation. Of course, your employee may disagree with your perception of the situation. You may see a gap, whereas the employee may not or may acknowledge a gap but blame it on others or on a lack of critical resources or on some other factors beyond her control.

For the counseling session to turn around the employee's performance, the employee must agree that a problem exists and that she is responsible. To do that, you have to have done your homework. This includes knowing how often the problem occurs and the consequences of the problem on the person's work or on the performance of the department as a whole. More important, you have to have documented your observations.

After you have raised the issue, you have to be ready to listen to the employee's explanation. To prompt her, you might say, "Tell me about it" or ask, "Is my understanding accurate?" or "Is there more I should know about what happened?"

Of course, there is the possibility of a misunderstanding, and the employee may be in the right. So listen with an open mind to the explanation. If you believe the employee, then the matter is over. If you have doubts about the employee's view of the situation, then you can tell her that you will look further into the matter, then get back to her. (Parenthetically, if the employee is lying, the knowledge that you will follow up with other parties to confirm her story will prompt her to 'fess up.)

CONFRONTING GLORIA WITH THE FACTS

In the case of Gloria, assistant to Charlie, a warehouse manager (see Chapter 5), there was actually a letter from a client who was annoyed enough by Gloria's brusque manner to write to the plant manager, Charlie's boss. There were also several other incidents that Charlie could cite based on the observations of other managers, like the occasion when Gloria was seen reading a Danielle Steele novel while the other assistants in the plant were rushing about to complete a last-minute order, or the occasion when Gloria refused to help a coworker process an order while this other assistant completed an important report due out that morning.

Because Charlie had been blind to the existence of a problem until it was brought to his attention by the results of a 360-degree feedback (see Chapter 5), he did not have a lot of supportive documentation. Still, he had enough evidence so that the issues he raised with Gloria were not subject to interpretation or argument. Further, since he had set standards with Gloria at the start of the year as a part of the company's evaluation process, he could point to how the undesirable behavior represented a major discrepancy with the work standards to which she had agreed.

Gloria continued to deny the existence of any problem for much of the meeting. She had been reading a book because she had "a terrific headache and needed to take a break" from a major project she was doing for Charlie at the time. She might have said no to the coworker who asked for help, but, Gloria told Charlie, she had her own work to do. "Can't I stop for a minute to catch my breath," she asked, "before someone with much less to do tries to pass her undone work on to me?"

Gloria then began to list the many tasks she was responsible for. Charlie had never complained about her performance before, and Gloria felt she could convince him that the complaints he had heard about her work were unfounded. Charlie sat silently and listened without interrupting her.

Charlie knew that listening to her comments in response to his description of the undesirable behavior was important to the success of the counseling process, especially in the earlier stages. It would not only demonstrate to Gloria that he wanted to hear her side of the story but it would also give him insights into the problems in her performance. He didn't want the meeting to turn into a confrontation; rather, he wanted a conversation in which he would play the smaller part—the 20/80 rule. He hoped that his silence would encourage Gloria to tell him about what was happening in the workplace, the problems she had, and why she was behaving as she did.

When Gloria had explained each of the incidents to her satisfaction, Charlie paused for about five seconds and then said, "I didn't realize that you were so busy. I can understand why you occasionally ask for help from some of the other assistants." Then he paused again, using silence to get Gloria to add more information.

"Well, it is true that occasionally one of the assistants lends me a hand," she acknowledged. "Work can stack up."

"I'm sure," Charlie answered.

"Are you telling me that I should be helping out if I have the time?" Gloria asked.

"What do you think?" Charlie asked. "Should you?"

"I guess I should," Gloria admitted. "But there are times when I just can't."

"Looking back," Charlie asked, "do you think those instances I mentioned earlier were times when you couldn't help because of critical work that had to be done?"

"No," she admitted. "I had work to do, but I could have put it aside to lend Linda a hand."

By asking questions and listening carefully to the replies—demonstrating his interest in her comments both by his remarks and by body movements like leaning toward Gloria and nodding his head—Charlie had begun to achieve his first goal: to get Gloria to accept the existence of problems in her performance.

As they talked, he was also able to communicate to Gloria the implications of her behavior both for the department and for her. The department was short-staffed, and everyone had to pull together if client firms were to get their orders as promised. Those members of the staff who acted as if they were above the team and didn't cooperate wouldn't get a raise, might even be placed on warning, and could be terminated.

Goal 2: Identify the Problem's Cause

Often the source of the performance problem isn't clear, as turned out to be the case with Gloria.

Gloria believed that, because she was the assistant of the warehouse manager, her work took priority over everyone else's. In her mind, this meant that she shouldn't be bothered with "nuisance phone calls from customers who didn't know what they wanted" or with requests for help from the assistants of those who reported to Charlie.

When Documentation Isn't Helpful

Charlie had not had much documentation to use to help him identify the source of the problem with Gloria. He had to use his first meeting with her to get her to acknowledge that a problem existed and to find its cause. But sometimes, despite much documentation of a problem in performance, it doesn't reveal the cause of the problem. Or a manager may assume that he knows the cause of the performance problem but, after probing beneath the surface, may uncover an entirely different picture from what at first seemed to be the truth.

Consider what happened to George:

GETTING INPUT FROM COLLEAGUES

The head of purchasing for a print house, he had decided to keep Lisa on when the company downsized his department. Now, six months later, he wondered if he had made the right decision about which individual to let go.

George carefully documented his employee's performance, and his records showed that Lisa took anything he said as a reprimand and became argumentative in response. She had also been in arguments with coworkers and other managers. Her behavior had become disruptive to the department, and he had scheduled a counseling session with her to discuss the problem and try to come up with some solution.

Over lunch, he met with Micki and Chrissy, two other supervisors at the Atlanta-based printing company. Since Micki had once supervised Lisa, George decided to use this meeting to ask Micki if she had any advice on how to open the discussion with Lisa. He would be meeting with her that afternoon for the first in a series of "unproductive counseling sessions," in his opinion, if he didn't get a better fix on the nature of the problem.

When George mentioned the situation he was facing, he found that Micki and Chrissy were in similar binds: Micki was already counseling Todd but to no avail, and Chrissy would begin counseling Bill next week. Todd was a workaholic, Micki explained, and he put a great deal of effort into his job. But he got too involved in minute details. He got so wrapped up in them that on two occasions major print jobs were completed behind schedule. Bill presented a different management challenge. He didn't care about deadlines, frequently came to work late, produced sloppy paperwork, and didn't care how he or his office looked. The following conversation ensued:

Chrissy: How do I tell an employee to bathe regularly? *(George and Micki laugh.)* No, I'm serious. When he came to the company, he was dressed in a suit and was at work a half hour ahead of schedule. Now I'm lucky if he's only a half hour late. And he seems to have one shirt and one pair of pants and to wear them each and every day.

George: I think I know what's wrong with Bill. His wife left him about six months ago. It could be that the poor guy is so devastated that he just doesn't care about anything anymore, including his work.

Chrissy: Do you think that's the problem? When I meet with Bill next week, I'll ask him if he's had any personal problems that could be behind his performance problems. If you're right, counseling may be worth the time. I thought I would just be going through the motions and would ultimately have to terminate him.

George: Well, ladies, what about Lisa? Do you have any idea why she is always on the defensive?

Micki: I would be frightened if I worked in a department that had just undergone layoffs. Say, that could explain her defensiveness. At least it's one issue that you can raise with her.

George: I will. Micki, I wish I could help you with Todd, but I don't know anything about him.

Chrissy had no inside information about Todd, either, but she had a suggestion: "Review his job with him." Chrissy explained how at her former job she had had problems because she had no clear idea of her job priorities. "I thought I was doing a super job, then I found myself in counseling and nearly terminated," she recalled. "Could that be Todd's problem?"

"It shouldn't be," Micki said, "but I'll make sure at my next session to go over the job description and make clear the priorities. Thanks for the input."

The three supervisors were able to help each other. During their lunch, they came up with three likely reasons that would enable them to better direct their counseling efforts.

Issues That Create Problems

Among the issues that can create problem performers, and that you should consider when you have to counsel an employee, are:

◇ *Stress.* Sometimes the stress comes from the demands of the workplace. Sometimes it can come from factors outside the workplace.

◇ *Unclear priorities.* Where this is the problem, the responsibility is more the manager's than the employee's. While the employee should have verified his assumptions about what demanded priority, the manager should have made clear from the first day the individual was on the job which tasks took precedence.

◇ *Poor time or task management.* Some employees are more skilled at organizing their work than others. Those who lack the ability can easily become overwhelmed in today's leaner organizations in which they get multiple assignments, each of equal importance. Often, though, all these individuals need is some training in setting priorities, planning, and organizing their time.

◇ *Oversupervision or undersupervision.* Oversupervision can make an employee, particularly a creative one, feel thwarted, unable to pursue her ideas without first clearing them with her supervisor. In economic downturns, oversupervision can also make some employees feel that their bosses are just looking for justification for terminating them.

If the problem is undersupervision, the employee may not know how to get done what she has to finish.

◇ *Interpersonal conflicts.* Conflicts may be between employees on the same level or between the employee and you. The resolution is mediation, either by you, or, if you are a party to the conflict, by a third, objective person.

◇ *Breach of promise.* Dissatisfaction with the job and company may begin right after an employee is hired if, during the interviewing process, the employee has been led to believe that the job he is being considered for is one with more responsibility or promotion opportunities than it really has. Maybe the promises were well intended, but circumstances beyond the manager's control now prevent him from making good on them. The cause doesn't matter, but the end result is a dissatisfied employee who takes his dissatisfaction out on coworkers and customers and by doing a second-rate job.

◇ *Personal problems.* It's difficult to do any job as we should when our personal life is a mess. The personal problems of a problem performer may be of the employee's own making or they may result from a problem of someone close to him. Regardless of the cause, it distracts him; at worst, it makes the employee unproductive and argumentative and uncooperative. Where the personal problem involves substance abuse, it could cause chronic tardiness, absenteeism, high accident and injury rates, or mood swings that make it difficult to know this person's emotional state on any one day.

Getting to the source of the problem, like getting acknowledgement of the existence of a problem, involves gentle probing and active listening. Most management textbooks leave the impression that counseling interviews are brief. You tell the employee she has a problem. She agrees. She comes up with a perfect solution, and you set up a follow-up interview. All done?—not so!

A manager has to take it slow and easy with some employees. For instance, George was right about Bill—his wife had filed for divorce and the breakup had so devastated him that he was now seeing a psychologist—but it took lots of questions to get Bill to admit the nature of the problem.

Counseling Bill, Todd, and Lisa

During her counseling session with Bill, Chrissy had no difficulty getting Bill to acknowledge the existence of a problem, but he hedged about the source of the problem. He just kept telling her that he was "taking care of it. Just let me have some time." Chrissy knew better than to blurt out questions about Bill's personal life, but what Bill left unsaid convinced her that George was right about a personal problem being behind the work problem. So Chrissy told him, "Bill, when I first hired you, you were extremely conscientious, concerned about exhibiting a professional image, and eager to take on more work to move up. I know you aren't happy with your appearance and the state of your work, and you are serious in promising to turn the situation around, but I need more than a promise that the situation will improve. What specifically will you do?"

That's when Bill admitted to seeing a psychologist to help him handle a personal problem in his life. Chrissy was silent, which prompted Bill to elaborate. He told her that he had started staying out late and drinking with some guys he had met at a neighborhood bar. He didn't like what was happening, but getting his license suspended for driving while intoxicated was the impetus for him to seek professional counseling.

Had Bill not been seeing a professional counselor, Chrissy likely would have advised him to consult the firm's employee assistance program or to seek outside counseling. Even so, as was necessary, Chrissy pointed out to Bill that while she sympathized with his personal problems, she could not allow them to affect his work or grooming since he worked in an area visited by customers. "If the problems continue, particularly your tardiness," she said, "I'll have to put you on warning."

Bill asked if he could review the status of several projects on his desk and come back with an action plan that would ensure completion of the work as scheduled. He promised no more late nights, and he would be in promptly at 9 a.m. thereafter.

Chrissy agreed to his offer, and she and Bill scheduled a meeting for Friday, three days off, to discuss the matter further.

Todd's and Lisa's Problems

Todd's problem turned out to be confusion about work priorities, and Micki was able in one meeting to address this by reviewing the standards by which his work would be measured. They were able to move quickly on to develop an action plan that would reassure Micki that Todd was clear about his work responsibilities and get him back to focusing not just on the details—the trees—but the forest, or department mission, represented in his work.

Lisa wasn't as easy a performance problem to get a handle on. From the moment she entered George's cubicle, she was uptight. George knew he would have a hard time with her. Normally taciturn, she did not stop chattering about her work from the moment she entered. George suspected that Lisa knew that he was unhappy about her relationship with him and other staff members, who were also targets of her sarcasm and defensiveness, and that she was trying to avoid discussing them by distracting him with talk about every job on her desk at that moment.

Finally, in the middle of a story about a requisition form she needed to complete updating her computer's software, George interrupted. Apologizing, he said, "That's all very interesting, Lisa. You obviously have your hands full. The layoffs didn't help," he commented.

"No," she said, now with a silence that was unnerving.

"It's been a tough period for all of us," George continued. "I wanted to discuss the impact it seems to have had on our relationship and your relationships with others in the department," George said, pulling out a log of his conversations with Lisa as he spoke. "I am concerned that you . . . ."

He hadn't even finished his sentence when the old Lisa returned. "You're always picking on my work," she said. "You are only doing it to get out of the promise you made me when you hired me," she continued.

Flummoxed, George asked, "What promise?"

"An upgrading and raise after six months if I did the job well," she replied.

"I don't think I made any promises," he replied. Controlling his own defensiveness, he continued, "During our interview, you said you wanted a job with promotability and I told you stories about two employees who had been upgraded after only six months with us. But, Lisa," he continued "we also discussed the fact that the job you were taking would involve stretch. After four months, we also downsized."

"You promised," Lisa replied, a grim expression on her face.

"Even if your work merited an upgrading, which it doesn't," George said, his calm regained only with difficulty, "there is no place for advancement. And I am very concerned about your behavior. You become so defensive when you talk with others about your work that several people have asked that I assign someone else to work with them instead of you. I have to agree with their complaints. You make it very hard for people to work with you."

George was again preparing to pull out the workbook in which he kept a record of his employees' performance, when she jumped up and told him, "OK, OK. I get it."

George wanted to move toward achieving the next goal in one-on-one counseling, but it was evident to him that he would get nowhere with Lisa until she had had a chance to think about what he had said. So he asked her to come to his office two days later to discuss how they could address her performance problems.

Goal 3: Agree on Specific Employee Actions

The third goal in one-on-one counseling interviews is to reach agreement on the specific actions the employee will take to improve performance.

GETTING AGREEMENT FROM TODD, BILL, AND LISA

Micki's single discussion with Todd had gone as described in management textbooks. Micki had said he wasn't doing the job she expected of him, he had agreed, and they had identified the cause as confusion about job priorities, and had been able to agree on what he should do in the future. He had signed an action plan that clarified his responsibilities. Problem solved.

On the surface, Chrissy also had done well. Bill had acknowledged his poor performance, Chrissy had learned the reason, and she and Bill had agreed on an action plan. Except that Bill didn't live up to the action plan he had signed off on. The very next day, he was late again to work. This time he was hung over. Instead of her session with him giving him reason to get back on track, he seemed to think that his disclosure of the problem meant she would let him get away with an "occasional night out with the boys while his divorce went through."

Scheduling Another Meeting

Chrissy knew another meeting was called for, and scheduled one with Bill that afternoon. George also had arranged for another meeting with Lisa. George's purpose was to reach agreement with Lisa on the steps she would take to make her work relationship with him and others better, whereas Chrissy's purpose was to formalize the actions she expected from Bill to ensure that he arrived on time each day, continued counseling, and caught up on his backed-up assignments. She also had to make clearer to him the consequences if he continued to come to work late and allowed his work to fall behind.

Lisa seemed more positive when she came into George's office. And with cause. She had considered the various opportunities in George's area and she proposed that he put her in charge of vendor quality assurance, which would guarantee her an upgrading, if not a salary increase. She attributed all her performance problems to his failure to keep his promise, and said that the upgrading would put an end to the problem since she would be working with clients, not envious coworkers or tradition-bound managers (which, based on her expression, included him).

George was shocked. While he could transfer her to another department with a vacancy—and get her an upgrading in the process—he knew he would only be passing along the problem to another manager. So he repeated his previous statement that there were no opportunities for advancement in the department, that she was not qualified yet for promotion in the department even if there was one, and that her behavior with others inside and outside the organization had to improve or he would have to put her on warning. To win some cooperation from her, he offered to provide learning opportunities for her by sending her to a course on purchasing if her interpersonal relations with others improved over the next six months.

Lisa was clearly annoyed, but this time she did not run off. She listened and grudgingly signed off on the action plan that called for her to be more responsive to others' suggestions, work more collab-oratively with others, and work to build bridges she had burned with others in the organization. They agreed to get together in two weeks provided another incident involving him, a colleague, or client did not occur in the interim.

George took a deep breath when Lisa left. He suspected that further problems might occur, but he also expected that she would begin job hunting. Given her attitude, and that attitude's impact on her behavior, he decided to call Human Resources to find out if he could put her on warning if another situation occurred.

Chrissy was more sanguine about her meeting with Bill. She laid down the rules to Bill—and much more firmly than she had in her earlier meeting. She made clear to him that he would be put on warning if he was late again, which was one step short of termina-tion. She would do this, she told him, if he didn't get his act together. She made clear that his personal problem did not give him an excuse to pull down the productivity of the rest of the department.

Before going on to the next goal, let me add one point about achieving this goal. Don't fall for the "I'll try" game, a game Bill was very good at.

When Chrissy asked him to correct his behavior, he kept say-ing, "Sure, Chrissy, I'll try."

When an employee says, "I'll try," he has agreed to the action plan but only to the extent of trying to achieve it. And *trying doesn't count.* If you are ready to close the meeting, and the em-ployee keeps saying, "I'll try . . . I'll try . . . ," you may want to move beyond that imprecise promise to get the employee to actu-ally state what he will do to make the action plan a reality.

Goal 4: Follow Up

You want to be sure that the employee is making the goals you both set. It's usually done at a follow-up meeting scheduled during the first meeting.

THE FOLLOW-UP MEETING

Chrissy and George had both set up follow-up meetings in two weeks, whereas Micki had agreed to meet with Todd in a month.

Surprisingly, it was Micki who had to get together with Todd before the scheduled time. Rather than delegate to the department assistant some work for a proposal to produce a major publisher's new magazine, Todd had done the work himself, lost time in completing the proposal as a consequence, missed the deadline for submitting the proposal, and lost the client for the firm.

Since the agreed-on action plan between Todd and Micki called for Todd to delegate as much detail work as he could in order to complete bids and other proposals on time, his failure to complete the project on schedule was cause for a meeting between the two. Although he had acknowledged a problem at the start of counseling, this incident, more than the earlier discussion, brought home to him how important it was for him to delegate the details to others. He promised that there would be no repetition of such an incident, and Micki felt that he meant it. But she made clear to him that, given the importance of his work, a repetition would put him on warning.

A few days later, Chrissy met with Bill to discuss his progress. Since their second meeting, Bill had not been late. She also learned then that Bill had caught up on almost all his work. After their second meeting, Bill had provided Chrissy with a report on the status of his work. At this follow-up meeting, he showed Chrissy that, except for one major task, all other tasks had been completed. He had done so by putting in hours at the office after others had left.

He also informed her that the divorce papers had all been signed, and he and his psychologist had agreed that he did not need further professional counseling.

Chrissy reminded him that he was still in performance counseling, but she also told him how pleased she was about his efforts.

George continued to have it harder than Chrissy and Micki. He had to put Lisa on warning for losing her temper with one of her coworkers who had moved some files. Once again, Lisa blamed George for the circumstances in which she found herself. He had seen the human resources department, and received its assurance that so long as he documented each of his meetings with Lisa he would be within his rights to terminate her if another such incident occurred. The warning memo that Lisa left with made that very clear.

It stated that on several occasions she had been rude to coworkers and clients and had made it difficult for others to work with her.

It noted that she had met twice with George and had agreed to change her behavior, as evidenced by her signature on the agreed-upon action plan, but the problem continued. The circumstances that warranted the warning were also described.

Goal 5: Reinforce Improved Performance

You have to acknowledge improvements in an employee's performance to sustain that improvement. Toward that end, you might even want to reward the employee with a special assignment or opportunity for special training.

TODD, BILL, AND LISA: THE OUTCOMES

The latter is what was offered Todd. To ensure that he no longer got so caught up in detail that he didn't make deadlines, Todd asked Micki if he could take a management course with a major emphasis on delegation. Bill was the old Bill again, on time and ahead in his work.

What about Lisa? She was true to her personality. She got into an argument over the telephone with a vendor rep, one of the most congenial people that the firm worked with. So she was fired.

Gray Issues

Let me share with you one other management story. It is important because it reflects a reality of counseling, which is that counseling can become much more complex than the issue of good or poor performance. Sometimes there are factors beyond the employee's willingness and efforts to change her performance that will influence the decision about the amount of time she is given to improve. For instance, you might find yourself being pressured by your boss or others in the organization to transfer, demote, or even terminate an employee with a remediable job problem because he lacks the skills to handle some new office technology. The assumption is that it is more efficient for you to hire someone better skilled than it is to spend time training the problem employee. But is this true, or fair?

Sometimes the pressure is due to such an amorphous situation as senior management's belief that the problem performer just "doesn't fit in." That's what happened to Mel.

MEL'S DILEMMA

A manager in a consulting firm based in a small town in New York State, Mel had an assistant named Donna. When Donna moved out of her family home and got her own apartment, she started to come in late despite the nearness to work of her new residence. In addition, she began to take extended lunch hours. Mel tried to be understanding, but after a month of this behavior he decided to talk to her about her late arrivals and long lunches. She wasn't that late for work or after lunch, but she wasn't there to pick up the phone and the company did not have voice mail. Like most managers, Mel spent much of his time in meetings with colleagues or clients.

Mel's Boss: A Complicating Factor

Mel felt that all he would have to do would be to remind Donna of her responsibility to be on time for work and after lunch, and the problem would be solved. But Mel's boss, Sid, wasn't so happy about this solution.

Truth was, Sid didn't like Donna. Her funky clothes and bright-orange-colored hair didn't fit his image of an administrative assistant for Mel, one of the firm's top—and most highly paid—consultants. Sid's own assistant had a sister, and he suggested that Mel use the chronic tardiness and long lunches as a way to rid himself of Donna and get someone like his secretary's sister, someone who looked and dressed the part of an assistant to a high-priced consultant.

Mel felt himself caught between a rock and a hard place when he learned that Donna might need to go on flextime and take extended lunch breaks for a few more weeks, if not months. She had a new puppy, and she was having problems housebreaking him. Mel explained the situation to Sid, but it carried little weight. "Tell her she has to get in on time," he said, "even if she has to get rid of the pooch." Obviously, he hoped that Donna would choose the dog over her job.

Mel had no intention of suggesting to Donna that she get rid of her new dog. Nor did he want to lose Donna, who had worked for him for several years, knew him and the firm's work well, could anticipate the needs of clients when they called, and, maybe most important, was very organized, making up for his own disorganization.

On the other hand, Sid kept pressing for Donna's dismissal.

A Showdown With Sid

Finally, Mel had it out with Sid. He admitted that there was a problem; he also believed that there were some problems with Donna's professional image. He would discuss all this with her, and they would try to reach some compromise, but he would not insist that Donna wear only business suits or recolor her hair to a less vibrant hue. About her lateness, Donna had arranged to have a coworker at a nearby workstation pick up the phone on those days that she was late for work. She would make up for her tardiness by taking work home. As far as her extended lunch hours to check on the pup were concerned, she had talked a neighbor into doing this and walking the dog if need be. Most important, Mel pointed out the cost to the company of losing Donna—not only in terms of her knowledge but in real dollars spent for the high-priced temp who would be necessary until a full-time replacement could be found, for a recruitment firm to find a suitable candidate, and for the higher salary the company would have to pay a newcomer who would demand far more than Donna was currently earning.

Mel made a strong case for helping Donna work out her problems. And his arguments were all valid. Before giving in to pressures—whether from an increasing workload or from clients, colleagues, or even your boss—you should weigh the time you will have to invest in finding a suitable replacement for the job and the cost of recruitment, including training time and the lowered morale of staff members who will mourn the loss of their coworker, against the return on counseling, which could include not only improved employee performance but increased employee loyalty and commitment and growing managerial respectability among staff members. Remember, too, that there is no guarantee that the new hire will not have any performance flaws.

Summing Up

What do the experiences of managers Charlie, George, Micki, Chrissy, and even Mel tell us about the counseling process?

◇ You can't get far in counseling unless the employee accepts the existence of a problem.

◇ You should be clear about the purpose of the meeting.

◇ You need to describe clearly the undesirable behavior and to be able to show, through documentation, the discrepancy between the standard or desired behavior and the current level of performance.

◇ You should be prepared for the employee to try to distract you or otherwise try to control the meeting rather than address the need for counseling.

◇ You need to probe the answers given in order to get a clearer idea of the cause of the problem.

◇ You should ask open-ended questions to get the employee to share his or her feelings.

◇ You should paraphrase the remarks of the employee to show that you are truly listening to what he is saying.

◇ If you must, you may want to prepare a list of questions in advance to ensure that your conversation is focused.

◇ You should encourage the employee to identify several alternative solutions to the problem and to share her feelings about the consequences of each of these alternatives before settling on a single plan.

◇ You should learn how to use silence to get an employee to fill in the silence with the critical information you want.

◇ You should give the employee the chance to tell his story without interruption.

◇ You must be sure that the employee knows both the effect of her behavior on workflow and coworkers' performance and the consequences of a continuation of the problem.

◇ You need to be clear about the kind of behavior or level of performance you want from employees. Make sure that you ask for behavior-related change, not attitudinal change.

◇ Don't reprimand. The more at ease the employee is, the more responsive he will be during counseling.

◇ You want more than a signature on an action plan as evidence of a commitment to change; the only commitment that counts is the actions of the employee.

◇ Don't make judgments about employees, like calling them "lazy," "difficult to work with," or "losers."

◇ You should show confidence in the employee's ability to turn around her performance.

◇ Be prepared with information about the company's policies and procedures (or ready to get such information) to help the employee come up with an action plan.

◇ Refer the employee to the employee assistance program or human resources department if the problem is beyond your scope.

◇ If the source of the problem is a personal problem, while referring the employee to others, aim for agreement on actions he will take to turn around his performance.

◇ Recognize that there may be factors beyond the individual's performance to include in any equation concerned with salvaging the employee.

If you are to turn around a problem performer and get good to outstanding performance from him, you have to demonstrate that the employee can't just go through the motions when in counseling. And the only way you can do this is to prove by your actions that you are prepared to move up to the next step in the counseling process—through the warning stage to termination—if the employee doesn't improve in very specific ways. So, after that first meeting, monitor his behavior, praising even minor improvements as an incentive for him to make greater efforts.

If there is no change by the end of the agreed-upon time, find out from the employee why he thinks the problem continues. Consider new options, such as additional training or more frequent monitoring in critical areas, to help him overcome difficulties. Get his commitment to the new plan and set up a new date for evaluation. If the employee's performance rises to a satisfactory level by then, praise him, and if you think it is justified, consider some positive reinforcement, like a desirable assignment or a new responsibility to show your faith. But if the employee's performance doesn't improve significantly within a reasonable amount of time, it's time to talk warning, demotion, or termination.

So long as you can answer yes to each of the following questions, you have no reason to feel guilty about your role in the counseling process.

⋄ Did I give the employee the opportunity to share with me all the information about the situation?

⋄ Was I clear about the specific behavior that needed to be corrected?

⋄ Did I ask open-ended questions followed by closed-ended ones to get to the heart of the situation?

⋄ Did I explain both the reasons why the behavior change was necessary and the consequences if no change occurred?

⋄ Did I offer to help to ensure the change?

⋄ Was I clear that I expected the individual to meet minimum standards, regardless of her potential?

⋄ Was I ready to provide positive reinforcement if there was a change in performance?

⋄ Was I as fair as I could reasonably be to the employee, not allowing external factors to influence my assessment of his performance?

Chapter 7

Team Counseling

In your role as team leader, you don't only act as a coach. You also may have to act as counselor, intervening when problems arise that could hinder the team from achieving its mission.

Members of high-performing teams are committed to their team's mission and operating guidelines. They complete their assignments on schedule, as promised. They are open-minded about other members' ideas, not antagonistic. They are sensitive to their coworkers' needs and feelings and they don't allow differences in opinion to influence the respect they show their colleagues. They confront issues, but they do so without being offensive; they may question another's ideas, but they don't allow themselves to question another's professionalism or personal worth simply because this person holds an opinion different from their own. Finally, they keep their differences of opinion within the meeting room.

When There Is Cause for Concern

Members who exhibit behavior the opposite of this demand an immediate response by you as team leader. Otherwise, the team's mission is likely to be sidetracked, if not derailed entirely. Actions by members that demand your attention include:

◇ Failure to arrive on time, regular early departures, or chronic absenteeism
◇ Lack of preparedness for meetings or work not done by its due date

◇ Lack of interest in the team's work
◇ Frequent and unapologetic interruptions of other members when they are speaking
◇ Sarcasm or ridicule targeted at another member
◇ Refusal to hear out another member because of prejudice or narrow- or closed-mindedness
◇ An assumption of superiority over the other members or efforts to dominate the discussion
◇ Misuse of positional or political power to get one's own way rather than resolve the problem on the table

Both positive and negative behaviors fall into two categories: (1) behavior that is related to the team's work itself—from discussion of the nature of the problem being addressed to the brainstorming of solutions, to follow-up on ideas outside the meeting room, to follow-through and implementation of the final solution or plan; and (2) interactions that occur among members both within and outside the meeting room as a function of the team process. As a team leader, your responsibility is to monitor both and to intervene when problems either with the work itself or the process hinder the team's progress. This isn't easy in cross-functional teams, where you usually have no organizational authority over your team members.

Let's Get Real

When you are leading a team of your own employees, counseling the members is easy because you have positional power to add authority to your critical comments. Because you are their boss, your staff members know that they will be appraised on the basis of both their individual performance and their participation in the teams you lead. Consequently, if they accept your counsel as to their individual performance, they will accept your feedback as to their team participation.

Such agreement isn't as likely when you give your peers feedback. Unless your organization offers team compensation, and you as well as other members can influence the amount of the rewards each of you gets, or as leader you can have input into fellow members' performance appraisals—which puts you in the unenviable position of tattler if a problem exists, a role that won't win you much support from other team members if the word gets out—you really have little power over your team's members.

You can threaten to remove a member from your team, but would you? Taking such an action can, at the least, slow the team's progress as the individual's replacement (assuming you can find one) attempts to catch up with the group, and, at worst, it can factionalize the team as members divide their loyalties between you and the former member.

Before following through with your threat, you may even have to lobby for support from the rest of the team for permission to replace the member. Depending on the ground rules by which the team operates, you may not have the authority to make such a decision on your own.

Just as most management books provide a simplistic picture of employee counseling, so too do books on team management talk about team counseling. The truth is, without positional power over your colleagues, counseling team members about their behavior is tantamount to your saying to the colleague, "I'm right and you're wrong."

So, when counseling peers, you need to make a point of not sounding self-righteous. This would only alienate them when what you want to do is to get their cooperation, appreciation of the consequences to the team's mission of their continued misbehavior, and agreement to an action plan that will change the situation. If they accept your assessment of their behavior and readily agree to your recommendation, you're home free. You've done your counseling job. But it isn't always as easy as that. Not all your team members will be team players, willing to cooperate and accept and act on the feedback from someone who is *just* a peer.

In such situations, you may need to strengthen your words, and invoking the ground rules you set when you first assembled the team is one way you can do so. If the individual's behavior violates the team's guidelines, you can point that out, thereby strengthening your argument for a change in the person's behavior. Likewise, you can address those who lose team focus by reviewing the importance of the team's mission.

If you are familiar enough with your team members to know

what matters most to them (think "motivator"), then you can use these drivers to get them to behave more productively for the team's sake.

Finally, you can utilize peer pressure, giving the individual insight into how his or her teammates might be responding to the situation and how this could affect future relationships with these individuals.

First to the Basics

Most often, when we discuss the counseling role of team leaders, we talk about the team process and the need for the leader to step in when one member dominates the discussion, shows disrespect to another member because of something the other member has said, or otherwise obstructs an open and collaborative discussion. But even before addressing these interpersonal issues, there are more basic problems that should be considered: You might find it hard to believe that something as simple as chronic tardiness or frequent absences, or missed assignments, can so demoralize a team that it could fail to achieve its mission, but it is so.

One of a team's ground rules should be that meetings will start on time and that members will be responsible for alerting the group if they can't attend, and that members will be given tasks and expected to complete those tasks on the due dates set. These rules might seem too mundane to spend meeting time on, but many teams fail because of their members' failure to adhere to such simple guidelines.

The following case study shows how a single team member can disrupt the group by not following the ground rules and what a team leader can do to resolve the problem.

TED'S PUNCTUALITY PROBLEM

When Jekyll Apparel formed a new product team, Jill, its leader, worked with the group to set operating ground rules, including the need for members to be punctual for the start of each meeting. Still, Ted never seemed to be able to get to sessions on time.

Jill didn't let that cause her to delay the start of the meetings, which began on schedule. She knew how busy Ted was, so she never said anything, even though his late arrivals—usually fifteen to twenty minutes after the scheduled meeting started—tended to disrupt the group's discussion. Ted was responsible for developing the numbers for any business plans the group submitted, and he usually came loaded down with paperwork. While he got seated, and arranged his documentation on the table or on a nearby chair, discussion seemed to stall.

Was Jill right not to talk to Ted about his chronic lateness and its effect on the team?

A Spreading Problem

If the problem had been short-lived, maybe. But after a month, by which time Ted's workload had lessened, he continued to arrive at meetings late. On one or two occasions, he also came empty-handed, his assignments unfinished.

Jill saw also that Ted's indifference to being punctual, along with his laxity about his team assignments, was infecting other members of the team. Betty, Ken, and Marian, three other group members, also began to arrive late. It was almost as if they had synchronized their watches with Ted's. Half her team was now regularly coming in late. These same individuals began to let their team tasks slide, too.

Jill was upset but not as much as those members of the group who continued to take the operating guidelines seriously. Jill had seen some factiousness between the tardy and prompt members, but she had assumed it had to do with the proposals on the table; it had never occurred to her, until Bill spoke up, that those who had made a point of arriving on time were furious with the late arrivals, and that it was being reflected in the group's discussions.

"Do you know, Jill," Bill said, "over the last two months I figure I have spent about seven hours or a day's worth of my time waiting for Ted and his cohorts to arrive for these meetings? Why can't we just start without them?"

"Ted is bringing some key data today," Jill replied. "We need it to move beyond our earlier discussion of new overseas markets."

"You're assuming that he has done the work," Zoë said. Beside her, Julio nodded his head. Julio then rose. "I'll be in my office, Jill.

I have some correspondence to get to. Let me know when you want to get down to work."

Jill realized that she had a serious problem on her hands as Zoë and Bill followed Julio out of the room, mentioning similar small chores that they could work on until the group as a whole had assembled.

When Ted, Betty, Ken, and Marian arrived, they were surprised to find only Jill present. She called Julio, Zoë, and Bill into the room and the group got down to work. Fortunately, for Jill—and for Ted's reputation among his peers—he had completed his expected number crunching. But that didn't let him off the hook, in Jill's opinion. Nor were Betty, Ken, and Marian innocent bystanders, because they were emulating Ted's behavior.

Confronting the Culprits

Before the next meeting, Jill met with each of the late arrivers. As you can imagine, Betty, Ken, and Marian all used Jill's failure to do anything about Ted's chronic tardiness and undone assignments to excuse their own behavior.

"You're right, I should have talked to Ted about coming late to meetings," Jill admitted to Marian when she went to see her colleague. "But that isn't justification for your latenesses over the last few meetings. You also promised to have demographics for the team for both the London and Southampton markets. You're late with the information."

"Ted has been late, too, in the past, and you haven't said anything about it," Marian said in defense.

"Yes, I know. But we're talking about your commitment to the team, not Ted's," Jill continued.

"I . . ." Marian stammered.

"I know how busy you are," Jill said. "But the team needs your knowledge and support." Jill knew how important it was for Marian to be respected by her peers and it became her ace. Pulling it out, she said, "Your fellow team members will admire your contribution to the effort."

Marian started to defend her past behavior once again, then abruptly stopped. "Maybe you're right," she conceded. "I have been too cavalier about my participation in the new products group.

I will be on time in the future. And, Jill," she added, "I'll have those demographics for you by tomorrow. We can distribute them ahead of the meeting, so everyone will have a chance to study them before the session."

"Great," said Jill.

Jill also spoke to Ken and Betty. In Jill's discussion with Ken, she used the importance of the team's mission to his product line to get his agreement to change his behavior. Peer pressure worked with Betty, who was reminded of how angry she had been with a colleague who had never arrived on time in another team situation. "I can imagine how others on the team must have felt about my actions," she told Jill. "I've got a new computer program and I can use it to program my computer to buzz me when I'm due at a meeting. I'll be there next week on time," she promised. "Now for Ted," Jill began. She found him in his office working on his computer, and came right to the point:

Jill: Ted, I'm concerned about whether you have sufficient time to continue on the new product team.

Ted: Why do you say that?

Jill: You've missed several assignment dates and been late for almost every meeting.

Ted: Hey, what are you doing? Keeping records? Who do you think you are, anyway? My boss?

Jill: Not at all. But when you joined the team, you agreed to the ground rules that we all wrote. When you are continually late and don't complete team assignments on time, you're not meeting the commitment you made to the group when you helped us set those ground rules.

Ted: Others have been late.

Jill: Yes, I'm afraid that's because no one said anything; they thought it was acceptable. It isn't. We all agreed we would make an effort to be on time, be prepared, and attend all the meetings. As team leader, I should have said something to you. But I knew you were so busy with other tasks at the start of the project that I turned a blind eye to what was occurring. Now I have to ask you: Can you make our meetings on time? Otherwise, I will have to look for someone else to do your job. I don't want to do that if I don't have to—you're too valuable to the team effort—but I will have to find a replacement if you can't carry out your responsibilities to the group.

Ted stared at Jill for a moment. The two had been at logger-heads during several sessions of the team, but he had to admit that punctuality had been among the ground rules. He doubted that Jill would replace him on the team, but he didn't want to risk losing his presence in this high-visibility group. "All right," he said. "It'll actually help me to better prepare for the meetings. I can review my handouts in the meeting room just before the session starts to be better prepared to explain the assumptions on which they are based."

Jill's Only Mistake

Jill made one mistake in handling this situation: She waited much too long before acting on Ted's tardiness. Consequently, the problem spread to others. But once she faced the need to address the problem, she handled it well. She didn't use her position as team leader to demand that her peers change their behavior, with the implication that her role on the team would allow her to go to their boss or even the team's sponsor and complain. Rather, she used her knowledge of her colleagues and the ground rules set at the start of the project; she also reminded each of the problem team partici-pants about how he or she would be regarded by colleagues if they continued to violate the very ground rules they had agreed to sup-port.

Facilitating Discussion

As team leader, besides being concerned about the work being done during the meeting—which reflects how efficiently the time set aside for the meetings is being used—you will be concerned with the team process, that is, with how people on the team are interacting in discussions. Productive teams are those in which all members feel safe to participate in the discussion; they don't worry that their ideas or they themselves will be the target of more dominant members. When that environment is threatened, then you, as team leader, need to intervene.

In most instances, it is enough to use the same facilitation skills that you have taught the team as a coach to address the problem. One member disagrees with another's idea, even says, "Joe, I never knew just how limited your thinking was until now." You can interrupt the attacker and say, "Leslie, I don't think that's fair. I'd like to hear what Joe has to say." As the attacker looks at you, you can point to the operating ground rules that hang in the room to remind this member that she is stepping over the line that she herself helped draw.

But sometimes the misbehavior of a member during the discussion can require more than a reminder of the team's ground rules. Then you may need to take the member aside and discuss his behavior. Once again, since you lack positional power, you may want to refer to the group's ground rules, use peer pressure, or use your knowledge of the individual to convince him of the wrongness of his action.

OVERRIDING RUDE TEAM MEMBERS

Consider what happened to Toby, a warehouse manager who headed up a team at his plant to identify how to streamline product distribution and delivery.

On the team was one member who rambled on and on. Dan would get hold of a subject and, like a dog, hang on to it as if it were a meaty bone. Toby had found he could regain control of the meeting by waiting until Dan paused for breath. Then Toby would say, "That's an interesting point. Now let's hear from another member of the group." Because there were often nuggets of gold to be found among the slag, Toby had never spoken to Dan about his communication style.

One day, however, the situation came to a head. Millie, one of the team members, ridiculed Dan before the others.

Millie was new both to the company and to the team. She had quickly found a friend among the managers in Sylvie, and they both would smirk at each other as Dan floundered around, obviously amused at his inability to get to the point. At this team meeting, after a long statement from Dan, Millie began to speak, then paused. She looked at Dan and sarcastically asked him, "Are you through, Dan? Maybe you want to tell us, again, what you have just told us twice already? Or do you have something else to say to the group? I wouldn't want to take up your time."

Sylvie snickered. More compassionate, the rest of the team sat in stony silence. Dan's face turned bright red and he excused himself from the room.

Toby suggested that the group take a break and return to the room in about a half hour. Millie and Sylvie were leaving the room when Toby called them over. "I would like to talk to you both," he said.

Taking Millie to Task

Once in his office, he said, "Millie, I know you are new to the team. Still, your behavior was deplorable. You had no reason to insult Dan as you did. We all have little idiosyncrasies that our peers learn to tolerate. Dan is one of our most creative members. Admittedly, he doesn't know when to let a topic drop, but you were rude to him. If you want to win your fellow members' respect [peer pressure], you will have to be more sensitive to people's feelings. You are new with the company and want to make friends with the other managers [a motivator or driver]. I can't tell you to apologize to Dan, but I can tell you that you won't win any friends here if you get a reputation for being disrespectful of your colleagues."

Sylvie was another situation. After Millie had left, Toby asked her why she had been encouraging Millie's behavior. Sylvie denied any contribution to the incident, but, reading between the lines, Toby got the impression that more had prompted Sylvie's behavior than Dan's repetitiveness. She and Dan had both applied for a position within the company, and Dan was favored to get the job even though it included some public speaking.

Getting Sylvie's Cooperation

Toby personally didn't like Sylvie, but he knew she was important to the team's mission. He wished he could take her off the team, but that would only have created further problems with the group, several members of which were longtime friends of Sylvie. So he decided to take another tack to get her cooperation.

"I think you know how important this project is to the company," he began. "It will help all of us involved in the distribution of the company's goods. Your shipping operation, in particular, will benefit if some of Dan's suggestions prove workable."

"I guess you're right," she said.

"That's why I want you to head up a smaller group within the project team to investigate one of Dan's ideas more fully. If he's right, we should be able to get product to shipping at least a day or two sooner than we do now. How about it?" he asked.

Toby figured that Sylvie was hurting from the knowledge that she wouldn't get the promotion and that she needed to feel valued. Giving her this assignment would make use of her administrative skills and likely make her more appreciative of Dan's strengths and less critical of his weaknesses.

Toby could have reminded the two managers about the group's ground rules, but instead he used their need to be well regarded by their peers and to be appreciated for their contribution to the organization to get them to admit their misbehavior.

But Toby wasn't done yet. He had one more task before calling the team back together again. He had to talk to Dan.

Dan was in his office. "I guess I do go on, don't I?" he asked Toby, who was a friend as well as a colleague.

"Yes, you can," Toby admitted. "But you are one of the most creative people I know," he added. Then he observed, "When we first formed this team, we all went through team training. The focus was on problem solving and critical thinking. I didn't think that the group as a whole needed training in communication, but. . . ." Then he paused.

"You think I could benefit from such training," Dan said, finishing his colleague's sentence.

"Yes, I think you can," Toby said. Then, switching from his counselor's hat to his team coach hat, Toby suggested that Dan talk to the head of training about communication courses he might take to improve his speaking skills.

Kicking Out a Team Member

You may be asking yourself whether Toby could have taken more drastic action and actually kicked Millie and Sylvie off the team.

Yes, given the emotional response of the rest of the team to the twosome's behavior, he probably would have had their support for such action. But it wouldn't have undone the damage: Dan might actually have become more self-conscious about his speaking skills if he knew that Millie and Sylvie had been dumped because of him. And Millie and Sylvie would have been bitter and could have made implementation of any team idea difficult, if not impossible. And the team would have lost Sylvie's know-how and Millie's fresh perspective on the situation.

When should you kick a member off a team you are leading? When a member not only isn't contributing but is continually impeding the team. If you have talked to the individual not once but twice about his behavior and yet you see no change, and its continuation could very easily prevent the team from completing the goals it has set, then you are justified in asking a member to leave, either on your own or with team support, depending on your authority as the group's leader. Should you act without first alerting the team, then you will need to have a plan to replace the former member and also to be prepared to answer any questions the team may have about your decision.

Should you need team endorsement before acting, it is best to talk to one or two members first to determine whether or not the group will support the idea. If these individuals are agreeable to your action, and also promise to support your decision at a team meeting, then you can call the group together minus the problem participant and talk out the issue.

Sometimes the team may choose to keep the member but as a group remind him of his obligations to the group. If the unrepentant member continues to try to dominate the group, or is late as regularly as a commuter train, or discourteously jumps in as another member is speaking, or whatever, the team can come to an abrupt stop, and the unrepentant member may be asked by one of his peers, "May I give you some feedback?" The member then delivers the message that the team as a whole wants to communicate.

Let's say that Virginia always leaves meetings before they end. You met with her and discussed the problem, but it has done no good. The team now wants a chance to get through to her. "Virginia," a member tells her, "I may be wrong, but it seems to me that you would rather be somewhere else. I think this because you have left the last two meetings about a half hour before their end, and today you have spent the last fifteen minutes continually referring to your watch. I am uncomfortable about this because we have a complex issue on the table right now, and if you leave, we will be kept from making a decision until the next meeting. Even then, any decision we make as a group may be a mistake because you will not have been a part of the discussion nor will you have contributed to or heard the different viewpoints."

If you were Virginia, and you saw that the rest of the team was equally annoyed with you, would you leave early? Unlikely. In the future, you would also make it a point to be on time and to stay through team meetings.

Mediating Team Conflicts

As team leader, you may also find yourself in the position of arbitrator, mediating arguments that begin in the team meeting, escalate into personality conflicts, and continue outside the room. If you are a part of the personality conflict, then you will want a third, neutral party to arbitrate between you and the team member over the issue.

Disagreements during the team meeting can be healthy if they are channeled toward increasing members' understanding of one another and, with these new perspectives, toward increasing group creativity. But sometimes disagreements get out of control, fired by a history of past grievances one member had with another that makes the first individual sensitive to a remark from the other. Attention of the team's membership then moves away from the group's mission and to the two individuals.

As team leader, that's when you need to intervene. Since generally it is not the discussion in the meeting room but the perspective on the situation that caused the anger to fester and that ultimately led to the shouting match between the two parties, you have to look beyond the specific incident. To explain your role in mediating the disagreement, you can point to the impact a continuation of the conflict can have on the group's mission. Ask the individuals, "What do you think happened here? When do you think a problem arose between the two of you?"

In the calm of your office, you can get the two parties to identify what triggered the outburst and then to figure out how the situation can be changed. Again, question the parties to get their ideas, "How can you make things better between you?" As they answer, try to steer the discussion away from fingerpointing and toward ways of resolving the conflict. Your goal is to determine a workable solution that both parties can support. To encourage the two to give up their personal gripes, you might want to draw, once again, on your three helpful tools—the group's operating rules, peer pressure, and your knowledge of the two disputants. Point out how such conflicts are in violation of the ground rules and can jeopardize the team mission. Point out how angry words between them can ruin their reputations for professionalism among their peers. And, based on your knowledge of the two parties, remind each party of the merits of the final solution reached.

If mediation fails, you and the team may want to consider confronting the two parties in a group or, the tougher decision, asking one or both parties to leave because of their disruptive impact on the team's efforts.

Summing Up

When you put on your counseling hat as a team leader, there are six steps you need to remember. They are as applicable when you are counseling staff members on your team as they are in counseling peers.

1. *Describe the situation.* Refer to the facts of the situation. Even with staff members, you shouldn't be judgmental. But, in particular, avoid sounding self-righteous with a peer. Explain that you have to discuss the person's behavior because of the importance of the team effort and of that person's potential contribution to it.

2. *Listen to the other party.* Give him a chance to explain what has been happening. Show your colleague (or staff member) that you are willing to listen. Paraphrase what you hear and ask questions. Don't interrupt.

3. *Acknowledge the person's explanation.* This doesn't mean that you are giving her a license to continue the disruptive behavior. There are consequences to a continuation of the situation, and remind the team member of those. If she refuses to accept your right to question her behavior, pull out a copy of the team's ground rules. Or point to the impression that her behavior may be making on other members of the group. If the team mission or involvement in the effort is important to a peer or to her department, remind her, once again, of the consequences of her continued behavior on achievement of that mission.

4. *Determine the behavioral change needed.* Don't be pushy with a colleague. Or, for that matter, with an employee. Help him identify a solution to the problem by asking probing questions. For instance, if a peer has been absent more often than present at team meetings, and has not completed team tasks, ask, "Would there be some way that the team as a whole could free you to complete your team assignments?" If a staff member is late in completing a team assignment, you might question, "Is there another, higher-priority task? If so, we might be able to ease your workload over the short term to give you time to complete your team assignment."

As team leader, you shouldn't see a counseling situation as a battle that you have to win, particularly with a peer or colleague. You shouldn't want to prove you're right and the other party wrong—you want to find a solution to the situation that will be acceptable to the other party, ensure positive team dynamics and workflow, and keep the team's mission on course.

5. *Get a commitment to action.* The team member has to accept responsibility for changing his or her behavior.

6. *Provide feedback and support.* If it is a staff member, you might bring up the change in her team participation at the next evaluation meeting. If it's a peer, you would offer less formal feedback—maybe public praise for a job well done, a memo of thanks to be inserted in the person's personnel file, or just a smile when that chronic latecomer arrives on schedule.

Chapter 8

Counseling Traps and Problems

The traps associated with counseling fall into three categories. First, there are the traps and problems associated with counseling itself.

The second group of traps may be encountered as you move beyond counseling to the warning stage and the likelihood of termination. If the employee continues to misbehave or perform poorly, you will have to put the individual on warning and, if this doesn't work, terminate him or her.

Because some disgruntled employees may follow through with their threat to sue in the event of termination based on your "biased" assessment of their performance, the third group of traps is a legal one.

Some of these problems have been discussed in earlier chapters in this section of the book, but they are repeated here because they deserve emphasis.

Acceptance of Poor Performance

The biggest mistake that managers can make with problem performers—whether due to poor performance or discipline issues—is to ignore the problem.

You may realize that getting together with a problem performer to discuss the problem and develop an action plan to improve the employee's performance is the best thing for both you and the employee. Depending on the nature of the problem, such intervention may put the problem performer back on track or even salvage his career. And by intervening in this way you will come across to your staff, peers, and boss as someone who is in control of your operation.

But, given the problems that counseling can create and the time commitment it demands, it is easy to convince yourself that you are too busy now and can address the problem later (for instance, during the next appraisal review), or that the problem isn't serious enough for you to hold a counseling interview with the employee (you can handle the task that the employee isn't capable of doing or look the other way when he arrives late or leaves early regularly), or that the problem will disappear in time when the employee moves elsewhere within your company or to another firm. But are you only rationalizing your own unwillingness to confront the employee?

Ask yourself, "Do I truly plan to discuss this problem during the next appraisal review?" "Is that too long to wait to discuss the problem?" "Until the problem is solved, or the employee moves on, do I have the time to do a portion of this employee's work for him?" "Is it fair to expect all my other staff members to arrive on time and put in a full day's work for a full day's pay?" "Is it fair for me to put another manager, either within this company or outside, in the position of having to address this problem because I didn't?" And, maybe most important, "Who besides me knows about this problem?" Likely, your staff members, peers, and boss.

Management is the art of getting work done by others, and your performance as a manager will be measured by the performance of your staff, all of them—even your problem performer.

Failure to Get the Message Through

Often, when employees reach the warning stage, they argue that they had no idea that the problem in their performance was that serious. In some instances, it is an excuse; in others, unfortunately, it is because the employee's manager never made clear the nature of the problem and the consequences of its continuation.

So it is important that, during counseling sessions, you be very specific about the existence of a work problem and its nature, *and*, even more important, the consequences if the employee does nothing about it. Document your counseling sessions and share a copy with your problem performer, including the action plan you both agreed on to address the problem.

Disagreement About the Existence of a Problem

Sometimes an employee will deny the existence of any problem, and the manager will have to prove that one does, indeed, exist.

Unless you can point to specific incidents, a discussion with an employee with only a single performance problem can take the form of a "yes, you did"/"no, you didn't, prove it" conversation. This is where those management textbooks are right: You must document employee performance, both good and bad. As I will show later in this chapter, documentation of an employee's performance is important not only to defend in court any decisions you make about an employee but also to support your statements during counseling that there is a serious work problem requiring your attention and the employee's.

Documented observations also have the advantage of helping you during counseling to pinpoint both the nature of the problem and the steps to take to correct it. Mike, for instance, had an employee who did a spectacular job except for her behavior when working with staff from this advertising firm's art department. Carla, his copywriter, refused to accept Mike's statement that she always came into the art department with a chip on her shoulder. As he cited specific incidents he had been witness to, Carla found it harder and harder to deny that her manner made it difficult for the artists to work with her. Mike was then in a better position to find out the reason for her rudeness and come up with ways that she could mend fences.

If you expect the kind of opposition to your assessment of a problem such as Carla first gave Mike, you may want to have the records you have maintained on the employee with you and to have highlighted those incidents that support your remarks. If the individual's work is bad enough for you to consider putting the person on warning, you should also consult earlier performance reviews in which these issues were discussed. They prove that you have gone over these problems with the employee before. Have them with you when you sit down with the employee.

Disagreement Over Standards

Employees may agree that your assessment is accurate but then argue that the expectations, standards, goals, or outcomes themselves aren't fair.

You can counter this argument in two ways. First, if others who report to you have similar standards and have met them, you can remind the employee of this fact. Alternatively, if that is not the case, you can point out that over the years you and this individual have discussed the performance goals and at no point in the past did she raise this issue, as shown by your documentation of those earlier appraisals. With the appraisals readily available, you can even show the staff member that she signed the appraisal form or other document you use in your company's performance appraisal program agreeing to pursue these goals.

The ADA Excuse

Since passage of the Americans With Disabilities Act, many managers suddenly discover during a performance appraisal in which their employee is poorly evaluated that that employee has a previously undisclosed disability that is covered by the ADA.

After working with Marty for several years and tolerating chronic tardiness, Jack decided to do something about it and brought up the problem with him. Marty didn't deny that he was always late nor did he argue that other staff members also came in late and that it was unfair to come down on him alone. Rather, he told Jack that he had a sleep disorder, took medication that made it difficult for him to wake up when his alarm clock rang, and consequently couldn't do anything about being continually late. Jack knew his staff members well and kept his ear tuned to the department grapevine; yet he had never heard anything about

Marty having a health problem, so he doubted Marty's claim. Whether he believed him or not, though, he knew he had to hear him out. And if Marty did, indeed, have a sleeping problem, Jack would have to make *reasonable accommodation* for the situation. But Jack knew that he had the right to ask for confirmation of Marty's allegation, which he did. He asked Marty to bring in a letter from his doctor or to see the company's medical office. If Marty was an insomniac who had to take medication to fall asleep, Jack would accommodate the condition by putting Marty on flextime; Marty could arrive an hour later than his peers, but he would have to work an extra hour after they left. But being protected under the ADA didn't mean that Marty could get a full day's pay for less than a full day's work.

The Emotion Trap

Besides denying either your assessment or the validity of the goals, or coming up with a heretofore unknown illness, employees may respond emotionally to your comments about the need for them to improve their job performance. The responses run the gamut from tears to shouts to threats of violence. Some may show no reaction at all—they may listen quietly, then get up and leave—which can be equally unnerving.

The emotion trap is twofold.

First, knowing that your troubled or troubling employee will get emotional when you confront her about the need for improving performance may discourage you from ever bringing up the existence of a problem. Some managers would rather tolerate poor performance and even violations of corporate rules than have to stand before an employee who, they know, is likely to sob or, worse, shout at them or, worse still, threaten to go over their head to personnel or their boss or to take them to court or, worst of all, promise to beat them up.

However you expect the problem performer to respond, you can't let this person distract you from your course, which is to get her performance back on track.

Second, should an employee get emotional during a counseling interview, you should not let it sidetrack you from your mission, which is to get agreement with the employee that a problem in performance exists, what the nature of that problem is, and the actions you will have to take should the problem continue.

If the employee does cry as you expect, you can offer both compassion and Kleenex. Let the employee have some time to compose herself; you might even want to reschedule the meeting for later in the day when the employee is more composed or excuse yourself for a few minutes while the employee pulls herself together. Once you return to the room, you can begin by reassuring the employee that you would not want to begin counseling if you did not believe that she was capable of improving. You don't want to give the concerned employee the idea that the problem isn't important or that failure on her part to improve won't have any repercussions, but at the same time you want to create a climate in the room that will allow you both to discuss the nature of the problem calmly and objectively.

Shouts or threats about going over your head or to a lawyer should be handled professionally. Let the employee vent. If the person is out of control, you might want to suggest that you get together later when the individual has had a chance to regain control and you can talk more calmly.

Usually, after giving the issue some thought, the employee will return in a more subdued mood, ready to discuss the problem and set goals for improvement. At this stage, few employees carry through with their threats to go to a lawyer. At worst, they will go to your boss or Human Resources to complain. And if you have kept your boss informed of your situation with Employee X and alerted Human Resources about the need to undertake counseling, the employee will be met only with professional courtesy.

If you have the kind of hotheaded employee who might actually get violent, you may want a second person in the room with you. If the employee does hurl threats or suggests violent acts against you or the company, call security. Even if the situation doesn't escalate to the point that you feel physically threatened, you should report the threats to either Human Resources or your boss. And if you ultimately have to fire the individual, you should have a third person with you, even a security person nearby, should the worker try to make good on the threats.

Misunderstanding Your Role

Too often in the course of counseling, managers wrongly take on the role of sympathetic parent or professional psychologist. It's critical to maintain your focus as a manager—which is to get the employee to do fully and well the job for which he is paid—and to recognize your professional limitations. Not only are professional counselors better at identifying problems and helping individuals to solve them; they are also better at spotting phony sob stories.

WHEN TOUGH LOVE IS NEEDED

Zack had never been late until his mother was placed in a nursing home. Afterwards, he was late several days a week. Worse, Alice had noticed that he seemed a little confused and groggy when he walked in. She wondered if he was drunk. When she asked Zack to meet with her in her office, she raised the two issues with him. Zack told her about the pressures on him from working to save the family home and that he had had to visit a doctor for medication to help him cope with the anxiety he was experiencing. He denied he was drinking, since the doctor had warned that alcohol and Xanax—the medication he was taking—were a dangerous combination.

Alice believed him. As he sobbed out his story, she also found herself feeling extremely sorry for him. His situation reminded her so much of the situation she and her own brother had experienced when their father was placed in a nursing home. She was tempted to tell Zack that she understood and leave the situation at that, or to tell Zack about her family and advise him to see the same lawyer she and her sibling had used. Fortunately, she fought the temptation. She didn't let herself get so involved in Zack's problem that she was unable to separate her feelings of compassion for the hurt he obviously was experiencing from her management responsibility to ensure that all members of her crew were at work on schedule. Instead, she stressed how a continuation of his tardiness could lose him his job, which would only add to the pressures on him. She told Zack that she felt he had reason to be upset, but he could not use it to justify his chronic tardiness. She also was worried about the effect of the medication on his ability to work and asked him to visit his doctor to discuss other medications that would not leave him so drowsy during the day.

Instead of tolerating Zack's situation until he got his act together, as he asked her to do, Alice told him that she expected him to get his act together by Monday of the next week or she would suspend him for a week. She also wanted him to visit the employee assistance program and said she would make an appointment for him. They could suggest to Zack a financial adviser to help him get through his financial troubles.

Alice did give Zack the option of taking some time off to straighten out his affair, but he told her he felt better being at work.

For those of who you wonder what happened to Zack, let me tell you that he was able to find a lawyer who helped to secure the family home; he wasn't forced to sell the house he lived in. The government agreed that the property, while not in his name, was his sole residence and that he had maintained its upkeep since his father's death, when he moved in to keep his aging mother company.

Preconceived Notions

We may think that we know our employees well enough that we don't need to ask them the cause of a performance or disciplinary problem. This is a mistake. We should not enter into counseling sessions with preconceived notions about the cause of a problem, because we may be wrong. And if we are, this would mean that the action plan we set with the employee won't work. Besides, asking the employee the reason for a problem demonstrates that we respect his opinion and want to hear it.

Poor Counseling Preparation

With both troubling or troubled employees, you will want to have your documentation readily at hand to point to specific instances that necessitate employee counseling. With troubled employees, however, you also should have on tap information about your company's employee assistance program, if your organization has one, or, if not, community programs that might help the employee.

Failure to Consult HR

There are legal traps in counseling, as you will see later in this chapter. Consequently, it is unwise not to check with the human resources or personnel department before you schedule your first counseling interview with the troubling employee.

In your meeting with Human Resources, you should ask for a review of your firm's policies and procedures for handling poor employee performance or rule violations to ensure that you follow each step called for in your company's performance management effort. Failure to do so can make both you and your organization liable to a charge of discrimination.

Interviewing Traps

During the counseling interviews, there are other smaller mistakes you can make, like:

◇ *Dominating the discussion.* Here's where the 20/80 rule should apply: Speak only 20 percent of the time and listen 80 percent of the time. You also don't want to interrupt the employee; by doing so, you can miss some key point that will help you identify the reason for the problem.

To help you monitor how much you are talking, try this trick. During the next one-on-one meeting with an employee, note each time you speak and each time the employee speaks with a mark on a sheet of paper. Now compare the two. If you have more marks than the employee, you will need to learn to be quiet to give the employee an opportunity to talk.

You can check if you frequently interrupt an employee the same way. Mark each time you interrupt the employee, and each time the employee interrupts you, and compare the two records.

◇ *Shifting attention from the employee's performance problem to your problems or feelings.* You can point out how the employee's performance is creating problems for the department or organization as a whole, but you don't want to dwell on how his continued mistakes are making you look bad. Likewise, while it may be disappointing to have someone you trusted let you down or someone you believe has tremendous potential not use her capability, it shouldn't be the subject of the discussion.

◊ *Overempathizing with the employee's problem or feelings.* You may understand how the situation could have happened—you may even have been in the same boat once yourself—but you have to remain objective. If an employee senses that you are on his side, you are less likely to get a change in behavior.

◊ *Dictating what an employee should do.* For an action plan to succeed, the employee must be truly involved in its creation.

◊ *Moving too quickly into the problem-solving phase without first discussing the nature of the problem.* Doing this is really jumping the gun. As a result, the employee may go through the whole problem-solving process while still not believing that a problem in performance actually exists. As mentioned previously, the sine qua non of successful counseling is first getting the employee to admit that there is a problem.

Besides, the employee should have an opportunity to share her feelings. This will not only let her know that you care about her as a person but will give you a better idea of how successful your counseling will be. Listen not only to what the employee says but also to what she doesn't say; the latter is a "third ear" or counseling gauge, measuring how effective the counseling sessions will be.

Following Through on Your Warnings

Despite the quality of your counseling, not all employees will change their behavior or improve their job performance. At this point, the biggest mistake you can make is not to take the action you told the employee you would have to take if the behavior change did not occur.

If you don't act, you will prove not only to the troubling employee but to your entire staff that your warnings are meaningless, and they will act accordingly. Don't fall into the trap of holding one counseling session after another, after another, in the hope that the employee's performance eventually will turn around.

Different companies have different discipline and termination policies. But given today's leanly staffed organizations, it's unfair to you and your staff to counsel an unrepentant employee for more than two months before going to the warning stage. Remember that it only means extra work for you and a staff already carrying a heavy burden.

Even though you are at the warning stage, and the problem employee has acknowledged the existence of a problem, you will encounter some employees who will deny that a problem exists—he or she will look at you dumbfounded, surprised that, despite several counseling sessions, a problem *really* exists.

You can avoid any misunderstanding by making clear from the start of counseling that it is one step removed from warning and that warning is one step removed from the individual being terminated. Well-documented counseling sessions will enable you to prove to a third party as well as to an employee either in denial or lying that you both have discussed the problem over time. Memos to the employee should describe not only the nature of the performance problem but the consequences of its continuation—termination—and the performance standards or goals or outcomes that will need to be met to avoid those consequences.

From the first counseling session, you should set, and write down, targets for the employee to reach, in terms of both work improvement and the time by which the goal must be achieved. Be very specific in these targets. For instance, you might write about Marge, "By June 12, I expect you to revise the advertising kit." Or you might reach agreement with Will in customer service that "within two weeks, you will increase the number of callers you handle from ten to fifteen per hour." Further, because of previous complaints about his discourteous manner to customers, you might want to monitor his incoming calls and add to his target that "there will be no more complaints about being rude to customers."

If Marge claims that you never discussed the problem, or Will argues that you never suggested this was a serious problem, you will have in writing a summary of your discussion and the final conclusions.

Thus if Marge fails to finish the copy for the ad kit on schedule or Will continues to fall short of standard in the number of calls he handles and you have received another call about his brusque manner, you can place the employee on warning. This is the last chance—and you must clearly mean the *last chance* to turn around performance. Once again, you set a specific goal and timetable and put these in writing in a warning memo. And you provide the employee with a copy just as the employee received copies of the counseling reports.

When Termination Is Your Only Recourse

If the individual once again fails to make that objective, termination should not come as a surprise whatever the person might say. You will have protected yourself.

And you should feel justified in terminating the employee. If you have set specific objectives and the employee has done little to achieve those objectives or made only halfhearted efforts toward reaching them, then you need not feel guilty about having to use the three-word phrase: "You are fired." If your company has an intermediary warning step, you should make clear to the employee that this is his or her final chance to improve. A carefully worded memo to that effect should drive home that point. So should having to meet with you during the targeted period, during which you keep careful records of the individual's efforts.

Should the goals still not be reached, you will need to meet with the individual to terminate him. It's best to get right to the point. The less said at this stage, the better. Reiterate the nature of the performance problems that made you come to this decision and then send the employee to Human Resources where he will receive information about vacation pay or other benefits forthcoming and his legal rights. Despite the impact that it may have on workflow, it is better to have the individual leave immediately after he is terminated rather than give the person two weeks' notice.

Keeping the person on-site only opens you up to a fractionalized workforce as your staff members take sides between you and the terminated employee. Some disgruntled employees can also use their last days with the company to sabotage critical work.

There is much written about the best day or best time of the day to terminate an employee. Some experts argue against terminating anyone at the end of the week, on Friday, since it gives individuals two days to worry before they can contact potential new employers. These writers contend that in a tight job market, with few jobs available, depressed employees may harm themselves or others over the two-day weekend. Other experts write that it doesn't matter on which day you terminate an employee, but that it's imperative to do so at the end of the day, when there are few employees around.

I think it is more important that you treat the employee with respect when you terminate him. Keep the fact that you will be firing someone confidential, just as you kept the fact that he was on warning to yourself; the news will get out soon enough after your meeting.

During the termination interview itself, don't try to get even for all those times this individual created problems for you or the team or you had to do work that he was responsible for, and don't express sorrow that this person is not using the potential you recognize in him. Instead, use this occasion to wish the individual more success in the next job and tell him that he will personally be missed. Review in brief what has happened. Don't be long-winded; it can only trigger an emotional response or provide substance for legal action. Tell the employee something like this:

> As you know from our past conversations, we have certain standards in the company that have to be met. I think we approached those standards on a fair and reasonable basis. Over the last few weeks [or months], I have told you that your work has not been up to those standards. I don't believe it is because of lack of effort, but it just hasn't worked out. I don't think that it should come as any surprise to you. We're going to have to terminate you as of today. I really regret this. I had hoped that things would work out just as much as you did, I am sure. Human Resources can review what checks you have coming to you, as well as any unused vacation time. Susan in Human

Resources is waiting for you to call to set up an appointment
to discuss the situation.

If there is a security issue involved, you can have the person
watched, but marching him in lockstep to Human Resources and
then to his locker to pick up his belongings and treating him like a
convicted criminal can prompt him to lodge a legal complaint
against you and the firm and cause coworkers previously in agreement with your decision to change sides.

Dealing With Repeating Problems

With some employees, you may find that being put on warning is
sufficient to turn around their performance over the short term but
that the problem reappears after a few months. Angela was one
such person.

DEALING WITH ANGELA

Angela would sometimes be extremely passive during counseling
and yet, on other occasions, become extremely argumentative.
When Norm told her during counseling that he would have to put
her on warning, suddenly she started making deadlines, was on time
in the morning, took only an hour for lunch, and stayed until the
end of the workday. But once he took the pressure off her, she
returned to her old habits, slipping in after 10:00 A.M., taking ninety-
minute lunch breaks, and disappearing by 4:30 P.M.

And forget about meeting deadlines. Angela was apologetic
about the situation, but she would also get upset and argue that
there were lots of business reasons why she was behind in her work.
Still, she did nothing about these conditions that she blamed for
her work failures unless Norm, once again, threatened her with the
possibility of being placed on warning and terminated.

Norm tolerated the situation longer than he should have because he saw the tremendous potential in Angela. But in the end he
had to accept the fact that she was a lost cause, unwilling to use the
potential she had if she didn't have to do so.

It took longer than usual to terminate Angela because of her performance highs and lows, but maintaining a record of her inconsistent performance over nine months gave Norm sufficient information to make a defensible case for terminating Angela. This was a concern for Norm. One reason that he had not moved more aggressively to rid himself of her was that he was afraid she might sue for discrimination. She was over 49, suffered from diabetes, and had had a poor performance record over several years before she began to report to Norm, but nothing had been done about it.

Norm thought he would be walking into a legal minefield. Fortunately for Norm, Angela recognized the rightness of his decision and never went to a lawyer. But not all managers are so lucky.

Post-Termination Pitfalls

If an employee is terminated for cause but the employee decides to sue, charging discrimination, then you may find yourself in court defending your decision. There are four pieces of legislation that are often the basis for court cases:

1. *Title VII of the Civil Rights Act.* This act makes it illegal for an employer to discriminate against an employee because of the individual's race, color, sex, creed, or national origin. In 1991, this act was strengthened to allow plaintiffs to have jury trials and to sue not only for back pay but also for compensatory and punitive damages.

2. *The Age Discrimination in Employment Act.* This act protects employees and applicants more than 40 years of age against discrimination. In 1990, this act was amended to require employers to recommend that an employee over the age of 40 seek legal counsel before signing a waiver of employee rights and gave the employee twenty-one days to consider the waiver.

3. *The Vietnam Era Veterans Readjustment Assistance Act.* Under this act, companies with contracts of $10,000 or more with the government must take affirmative action to employ and advance in employment qualified disabled veterans and veterans of the Vietnam era.

4. *The Americans with Disabilities Act.* The ADA makes it illegal to discriminate against people in hiring, in job assignments, and in the treatment of employees because of a disability. In 1997, coverage was extended beyond wheelchair users, the seeing- and hearing-impaired, and drug and alcohol users to include the mentally challenged.

These laws were enacted to prevent discrimination, however, not to force managers to accept poor job performance from an employee in a protected group. For instance, under the ADA, an employer is required to provide, unless it is a financial hardship, *reasonable accommodation,* such as an oversize doorway to a cubicle or an access ramp for a wheelchair-bound employee or a Braille keyboard for a blind word processor. However, if the individual does not do his or her job despite the accommodation, then discipline and ultimately termination are within the law. Likewise, under the ADA, alcohol and drug users are considered disabled. But if such workers are found to be using drugs or alcohol while on the job or come to work under the influence of an illegal substance, you are within the law to take disciplinary steps leading to termination.

Some managers are so frightened of the repercussions of taking action against a poor worker within a protected group that they either ignore the existence of the performance problem entirely or go through counseling session after counseling session, hurling threats at the employee who over time comes to recognize how empty the manager's words are. But, in truth, managers only create a further problem for themselves when they do nothing: Coworkers who do their jobs resent one of their own getting away with chronic tardiness or excessive absenteeism, too much socializing, or missed deadlines, or whatever the job problem is. Actually, they see the failure to take action as a form of discrimination *against them,* since they expect you, as their manager, to respond with fair, understanding, and firm measures to correct poor on-the-job performance.

Left untreated, a problem employee's performance can cause you to be judged negatively by staff members, can set a bad example that others on staff will emulate, and over time can become a topic of conversation between you and your own boss. Then it becomes a problem with *your* performance, which can affect your career, if not threaten your job.

It's unfortunate that such situations occur. You should have little fear of legal reprisal *provided:*

◇ You have adhered to your company's policies and procedures, which in most instances means its performance appraisal program.

◇ You can demonstrate that you have applied the same criteria in assessing this employee as you have with your other staff members.

◇ You can prove that the standards or other measurements you are using to make performance management decisions about an employee are realistic and are based on the actual needs of the job.

◇ You have documentation to support your evaluations and final decision to terminate the employee.

When you allow a busy work schedule to keep you from conducting an appraisal of a problem employee, when you seem to be tougher on some employees than others and those on whom you are tougher fall into a protected group based on race, color, sex, and the like, or when you don't keep careful records of both positive and negative performance, you weaken your company's and your own defense against a charge of unfair termination.

Let's look at each of these traps in greater detail.

Failure to Adhere to Corporate Procedures

It doesn't matter how busy you are, you must closely follow the steps set forth in your company's appraisal program. If you treat one employee differently from another, you may open yourself and your organization to a discrimination charge. For instance, the company's policy may call for performance evaluations every three months, but you neglect to review one employee once out of the mandatory four times during the year. After all, you had to get that business plan completed prior to closure of the budget period, or you had to attend a meeting with visitors from another organization with which you are forming a joint venture, or you were invited to participate in a brainstorming session about a new product.

But let's assume that this one employee whose appraisal you don't get to is behind in his work. His performance continues to deteriorate. He spends all his time socializing with his coworkers, distracting them from their own tasks. He comes in late at least once a week. And he even talks back to you in front of other staff members. You meet with him and try to create an action plan to turn his performance around, but he denies the existence of a problem, blames you for demanding more from him than from the rest of the staff, and does not seem to care about meeting the goals you both had set at the start of the year. You put him on warning, but his performance still does not change. Ultimately, you have to fire him.

You conducted three of the four evaluations with him and have met on several occasions to discuss his declining performance, his behavior's impact on the work of the entire department, and the rudeness and disrespect he has shown you. Yet he charges you with discrimination because he, unlike his peers, missed out on that first quarterly assessment. His lawyer argues that he would have met the work goals if the problem had been caught sooner. He would have achieved his goals and behaved more properly if his situation had been given attention at the start. His lawyer tells the jury that you didn't give him the attention you gave his peers, not because you were too busy that week but because you didn't want to help him; the oversight was deliberate and attributable to a personal animosity or an age, race, gender, or other bias.

Even if the problem doesn't go so far as to lead to termination, you might find yourself in a court case. Let's just assume that the employee received a poor rating and no raise. He might go to the human resources department to complain or take the case over your head to your own boss. Finally, if he still doesn't get a raise, he might take his complaint to a lawyer and together they might take you and your company to court, charging that you deliberately discriminated against him.

Non-Job-Related Standards or Unrealistic Expectations

When you sit down with an employee and together agree on the standards or goals or outcomes by which her performance will be measured, you must set standards that are based on the actual needs of the job. This is required under the Equal Employment Opportunity Commission's Uniform Guidelines on Employee Selection. They require that standards be "valid" or "job-related."

A big mistake is to hound a talented employee who fails to use all her abilities. You may know that the person is capable of much more than the outcomes on which you've agreed, and it may be frustrating to see this individual not using her full potential, but so long as the employee is achieving the outcomes you both set, then the person is doing her job.

An assessment that reflects your frustrations can wind up in court and lead to a judgment against you at considerable cost to your employer.

Inconsistency in the Application of Standards

Just as failure consistently to follow your firm's policies and procedures can weaken your defense of a negative assessment of an employee, so too can evidence that one employee was allowed to get away with an infraction that another employee was not.

Let's say that an African-American employee was late three out of five workdays every week during the year. Despite your counseling and putting him on warning, he did nothing about his tardiness. In the end you terminated him, as you had several other workers of various races, genders, and ages. *Except* for one white employee who is chronically late yet has not been terminated. The terminated employee's lawyer could claim that the black employee might not have been terminated had he been white. And the plaintiff might well win his case.

Poor Documentation

You need to keep careful records of your employee's performance. When you can't point to specific incidents to justify a decision to pass over an employee for promotion or not to give her a raise, or to terminate her, the employee may charge you with discrimination and take your company to court.

Given your current responsibilities, asking that you document not only negative situations but also employees' accomplishments may seem too much to demand. In termination cases especially, it would seem to be enough to document negative incidents, but the courts question managers who can produce documentation only about poor performance or have only bad things to say about an employee. Critical incidents, good and bad alike, should be documented for all workers—poor, average, and outstanding workers.

That a manager has good documentation will discourage a lawyer from initiating a frivolous lawsuit.

What is good documentation? Certainly, it is not a notebook filled with empty phrases like "The employee was unable to follow instructions" or "The employee lacks motivation to do the work." These lend themselves easily to contest. The disagreement can land you in court, where you will be expected to prove your case by citing specific incidents in which the employee failed to perform to standard or didn't meet objectives.

Documentation should be such that a third party reading the record will be able to come to the same conclusion you have. This individual will come to that conclusion by reading your description of what happened, not by reading your opinion of the situation. Besides, at the time of the year-end appraisal, will you know why you wrote, "Barbara did a great job on accumulating customer records" or, more pertinent to the need for counseling or justifying a poor rating or termination decision, "Dan did a poor job in investigating competitive vendors to help us purchase our new office copier" or "Nan never coordinated the new format for company invoices with marketing"? Would you remember that Barbara spent long hours in the office making phone calls to more than one hundred customers to get e-mail and fax numbers or that Dan interviewed only two competitive firms rather than the five you asked him to consider prior to purchase of the new office equipment, or that Nan's failure to keep in touch with marketing led to several errors on the invoices as well as some omissions?

You want documentation that will support your case, so you should base it on your personal observations or, if the employee works with other managers as well, on these managers' observations too (think "matrix management" or "team participant"). Likewise, comments from customers or vendors will also help.

What if a manager or customer complains about one of your staff members yet refuses to go on record about your employee's poor performance? Unfortunately, you can't include the complaint in making your assessment of the individual's performance at the end-of-year evaluation and, consequently, in any documentation; actually, if the person sharing the negative observation refuses to be credited with it, its inclusion in the final assessment or any documentation can invalidate that assessment or documentation. Think that this is unlikely to happen? It happened to Phil.

PHIL'S STORY

Phil was a manager in a midwestern financial services firm. Alison was always complaining about Nancy, a member of Phil's marketing department, but because Alison refused to let Phil document her complaints about Alison's lack of cooperation in a team Alison led, Nancy's team participation never formed a part of her appraisals. Based on Alison's reports, Phil felt that Nancy deserved a rating of 2 (poor) or 3 (average), but because Alison refused to let Phil put her observations of Nancy on paper, Alison received a 4.

Without Alison's support, all Phil had was hearsay. And hearsay is not defensible. Even your own opinions aren't valid under the law. You may think that a person on your staff is a sloppy dresser, with unkempt hair and nails, but you can't write that in your critical incident report. On the other hand, you can describe that person's clothes and general appearance, point out that an important part of an employee's job is meeting with the public, and recount any comments from customers about the person's appearance that suggest how the individual's appearance is affecting customers' impressions of your organization or the person's ability to do her job well.

To avoid the documentation trap, it's best to keep two kinds of documentation: (1) incident reports that document specific events, the actions taken by the employee, the results, and the consequences; and (2) progress reports that evaluate the employee's problems and successes as he or she works on assignments or a team project. Training can also be included in the progress reports, as can incidents that over time show a shift (either for good or for bad) in work behavior. You can keep the critical incident records in a notebook that you update weekly, or you can create a computer file to maintain employee records, regularly backing up the record either on your company's network or on a disk.

Here are some other rules concerning documentation to follow:

◇ Document all counseling sessions, describing the behavior that prompted the meeting, the decisions reached, and the date for follow-up to discuss employee improvement.

◇ Give a copy of all counseling reports to the employee and place one in his personnel file.

◇ Should there be no improvement in the employee's performance, issue a warning memo that describes exactly the nature of the performance problem, past discussions about the performance, and the actions you expect from the employee and the time frame by which an improvement must be evident.

As with the counseling summaries, unless your firm has a special form it uses, you can use a standard memo format for warning memos.

Following these rules can ensure that your assessments of employees are fair and that you aren't accused of discrimination or arbitrary or capricious decisions about an employee, from giving the individual a particular rating to recommending him or her for promotion, to that tough decision to terminate an employee.

Counseling may be next to the toughest task that a manager has, with terminating an employee the hardest of all. But many managers may be able to avoid the need for counseling, and maybe even the need for coaching an employee, if they begin early by mentoring for performance management their average and better-than-average staff members. The third and final section of this book should help to get you started on this important task.

Section III
MENTORING

Chapter 9

What Mentoring Is All About

Any discussion of how to boost the performance of your employees must include mentoring, although mentoring is limited to your exceptional employees rather than something you do for all your employees, as with coaching, or only for your poor performers, as with counseling.

The Growing Interest in Mentoring

Mentoring is a topic that is getting much attention today. Ambitious managers and employees are looking for executives and other managers who will agree to help them up a career ladder that has fewer rungs than it had in the past owing to our flatter organizations. These individuals are searching for managers and executives who will cheer them on with "pep talks"; instruct them about the power and political framework of the organization; facilitate projects that they are working on by making both resources and contacts, inside and outside the organization, available; and influence the powers that be to promote them when a vacancy opens up. This is traditional mentoring with its focus almost entirely on the mentee's desire for advancement.

But mentoring has motivational value for you as a manager when you mentor your own employees, whether they are long-time, high-value employees or newcomers with tremendous potential. The same is true if you are a team leader and choose to mentor one or two of your best team members.

A manager recently told me how concerned he was that he didn't have the dollars to keep his best employees motivated and sustain their high performance. Mentoring is his answer and the answer for other managers in the same situation. Plateaued superstars will see mentoring as a reward in place of a promotion or a big raise. From your mentoring, your talented new hires will have shorter learning curves and be more productive sooner.

Under your mentoring, these talented newcomers will also be less likely to pick up bad habits from their less productive co-workers, assuming that through coaching you haven't been successful in obviating all counterproductive norms. Thus mentoring can be preventive, as is coaching.

In an earlier book, *The Manager's Balancing Act* (AMA-COM), I acknowledged every manager's right to ask of any business writer advocating some management action "What's the WIIFM *(What's In It For Me)?*" Increased productivity of your better and best employees is the WIIFM for you in mentoring staff members or team members. And mentoring doesn't have to be time-intensive.

Mentoring can be made up of one or two meetings so long as the message at these sessions is clear: You appreciate the superperformer's work and you care enough about her future growth and advancement to devote time to her career. These meetings send a message to your work team as a whole as well: Top performers and those who exhibit high potential will get extra attention. Thus you give your entire staff reason to push themselves further.

If your mentoring of one or two key performers has the domino effect within your entire department, you will get senior management's attention, too, and in the best way possible, as a manager who is able to get the very best from people and thereby contribute substantially to better, bottom-line results.

Mentoring vs. Coaching

Often mentoring gets confused with coaching because one of the functions of a mentor is to coach the protégé or mentee. But whereas mentoring uses many of the same techniques as coaching, mentoring involves *going above and beyond.* It is a relationship in which you do more than train the employee to do his job well. Rather, your focus is to share your experience, wisdom, and political savvy to enable your top performers to take on tasks beyond those designated in their job descriptions.

As a managerial mentor, your fourfold purpose is to be a:

1. *Role model.* Your behavior should be a model to emulate just as the behavior of the first Mentor was.

In *The Odyssey,* Homer tells how the adventurer Odysseus left his son, Telemachus, to the care of a servant, Mentor. For the next ten years, Mentor acted as the young man's teacher, adviser, friend, and surrogate father. He had less to do with teaching the young man the skills he might need in battle than with teaching him the values he would need to succeed as ruler of Ithaca.

About 1200 B.C., when Homer told of the siege of Troy, it was common practice in Greece for young male citizens to be paired with older males so that the young person would learn and emulate the values of the mentor, usually a relative. It was recognized what a powerful influence role models can have on a person's development.

Assuming that you practice the values you and your organization preach, your mentees are likely to practice these values too. When these values reflect the strategic mission of your department or the organization as a whole, you can expect the cooperation of your top talent in achieving these missions. Certainly they will be more alert to opportunities for achieving them and more willing to extend themselves to accomplish departmental and corporate strategies.

2. *Coach.* In this role, you help to clarify the organization's culture, political structure, and vision to encourage your employee mentees to correctly direct their efforts and avoid the political traps that could derail them from a fast track within the organization.

Mentoring includes being supportive of any ideas that the high-value employee/mentee might have on improving workflow or product design or sales. You have to be willing to be a sounding board for the employee mentee, acknowledging the strengths in his ideas but also helping him to see the weaknesses, to overcome these shortcomings, and then to develop a strategy for selling the idea to others with the resources to make it a reality.

3. *Broker.* Your employee mentee doesn't have the contacts you do, and as his mentor your role is to make these available.

You have listened to an employee mentee's career goals and you have served as sounding board for his ideas. Now you have to draw on favors owed you by peers to get the additional information or resources that the mentee needs to make his plan work. You act almost as a corporate uncle or aunt for the employee mentee, clearing the path for him to reach those whose approval is needed for the idea to be tried.

4. *Advocate.* You become a cheerleader for your employee mentees, giving them the chance to show others what they are capable of doing. As mentor, you recommend that your mentees be chosen to head corporate projects and otherwise give them the opportunity to advance professionally. The latter includes making the sacrifice of recommending a talented staff member to another company if there is no opportunity within your organization for advancement.

While you lose a top talent, in making such a move you let other talented direct reports or team members know that your interest in them extends beyond their day-to-day jobs.

What Mentoring Can Do for You

The first, and most important, decision you make respecting mentoring is whom you will mentor. Not only is it a matter of the time you will spend but other staff members will be watching you, and your selection of someone to mentor must seem as fair and logical to them as any other decision you might make about an employee, like a promotion or a coveted assignment. Otherwise, mentoring won't help spur other employees' performance. Unless your employees see in your mentoring candidate the same potential that you do, you could even be accused of showing undeserved favoritism or maybe even of discrimination.

In making your selection, consider the ten managerial benefits from mentoring one's own employees:

1. *Faster learning curves.* Taking a new and talented staff member under your wing, even for a short time, puts that person on a high-performance fast track.

2. *Increased communication of corporate values.* Not only will you be able to communicate the company's values—values having to do with quality of customer service, the kinds of relationships expected among coworkers, the sense of teamwork expected of everyone, and shared responsibility for corporate profitability— but you will be able to explain the strategic importance of these values. If you share with a newcomer how important these values are to the company's success, and, in some instances, to its very survival, the talented new recruit, with her fresh perspective, may come up with an idea for achieving one.

3. *Reduced turnover at a time when new recruits may be hard to find.* Right now companies have begun to pay hiring bonuses, even for entry-level employees in certain fields. Increased sales and profits have enabled managers to fill openings that they have had to operate around for several years.

Once you find a talented employee, and she has agreed to work for you, you want that person to stay. If you can't offer a bonus, you can promise her that you will set career goals and mentor her to enable her to achieve them. Having an adviser and friend in a higher position in a company can be more valuable than the financial compensation of a bonus after one, two, or three years with a company.

One-on-one communication between a manager and a talented new hire that shows every likelihood of continuing and that could include discussion of a role the new hire might play in future corporate plans can reassure the talented newcomer that he won't disappear into the corporate woodwork once the honeymoon is over. The individual won't worry about a lack of visibility and begin job hunting immediately after getting a job with you.

4. *Increased loyalty.* Mentoring efforts tell your employees that you care for them beyond their ability to complete today's work assignments. It lets them know that you are as concerned as they are about their future employability.

5. *Improved one-on-one communication and a sense of team within your work group.* Time spent with the mentee in which you

discuss your plans for his future can reduce the feeling of uncertainty the corporate grapevine may have created. Further, with your approval, your mentee can correct rumors that are demotivating the rest of the department and enhance communication within the department or division as a whole.

As you learn about group concerns from the mentee, you are also in a better position to focus on group gripes in team problem-solving sessions or other departmental meetings.

6. *Increased employee productivity.* The extra instruction that mentees get can motivate them to work harder, to take on challenging assignments, and to operate outside their boxes with some direction from you. Thus you tap the potential of your talented workers.

Mentoring is particularly helpful in maintaining the top performance of your superstars. These individuals can easily become frustrated when they realize that their hard work isn't going to get them quick promotions in today's downsized organizations. When that happens, they will quit. Worse than move on, they may stay but start doing below-standard work, qualifying them for counseling.

You want to give your top performers a reason to continue to outperform their peers. Your mentoring tells them that there is someone who is concerned with their professional growth and advancement; the personal coaching that will help them in their careers is a fair trade for their exceptional performance.

7. *More time for yourself.* Your mentees can take on projects that are important to your department or division but for which you don't have the time. You can pursue ideas that could increase your operation's bottom line while being assured that many of these more traditional projects are being handled. You can even delegate some of your day-to-day work to mentees since, in taking on this work, they are increasing their own skill levels.

Parenthetically, this use of mentoring works only if you monitor the work being done. This shouldn't be a problem because a major part of your meetings with mentees would be devoted to reviewing their progress on these assignments. Don't fall into the trap of many mentors and refrain from asking for updates either because you have convinced yourself that the employee won't have problems with the work—after all, you don't—or because you don't want to identify any causes for criticism.

8. *Additional corporate information.* The more information you have about what's happening in your organization, the better positioned you are to respond to your professional advantage as well as to the advantage of your organization's bottom line. Your mentees can see that you are kept informed of developments outside your departmental boundaries. Through their contacts with others in the company, your mentees become like listening stations, picking up key information that you might not otherwise be privy to.

9. *Creation of an innovative environment.* There is a very powerful, albeit subtle, relationship between mentoring and creativity. Mentoring, in essence, releases top talent to work outside their boxes. You, as a mentor, provide a safe, secure culture in which staff members can develop their ideas and innovations. And you see that they get the rewards their efforts deserve.

10. *Allies for the future.* Over time, as your mentees advance in their careers and gain influence within the organization, they can also be the friends you turn to for key resources or support for your own ideas.

Deciding Whom to Mentor

Knowing the ten benefits of mentoring, now consider your own staff. Do you have a talented but plateaued employee who could get off that plateau if she had stronger interpersonal skills? Maybe she needs to take a course or two or have an opportunity to participate on a team in which she can practice her skills? Or you might have a top team member who could speed the team effort if he had project management skills. Should this person take a CD-ROM training program in TQM techniques? Does that newly hired talent need a better understanding of corporate values or the department mission? Or does one of your more talented staff members have an idea for a new product and need you as advocate to get the critical resources to make the idea a reality?

How a Mentoring Relationship Develops

Most traditional mentoring relationships begin informally—usually after a request by the less senior person, albeit not necessarily the younger person, for advice or counsel or for resources to complete a project. But since you plan to use mentoring to boost employee performance, you will need to take the initiative. The next time the employee you want to mentor comes with a question, problem, or need, you should offer to be available to help the individual on a regular basis. An affirmative response would signify the beginning of a mentor relationship.

Make a commitment to meet with the employee one or two times a month to discuss his progress as team leader and to offer suggestions based on your own experience on how to get critical resources; or to discuss with another employee her efforts to streamline work processes and to share your political savvy on getting cooperation from key managers.

Let's look at a typical mentoring relationship and how it develops: the case study of Bob and Faith.

BOB AND FAITH: THE MENTORING RELATIONSHIP IN PRACTICE

Faith had been hired as administrative assistant to the head of purchasing, Bob Miller. Faith had held only secretarial positions before she applied for the administrative assistant position in Bob's department, but Bob was more than willing to hire Faith for the job. In his opinion, based on her training, previous job experience, and accomplishments in past jobs, Faith not only was qualified for the vacancy but ultimately could move up to assistant purchasing manger if she applied herself.

Bob decided to give her assignments that better reflected her capabilities than her job title, and in each instance she excelled. Each of these projects required stretch on Faith's part, and she recognized that. So one day she asked Bob if she could come to him if she ran into any problems with her assignments.

"Of course," he said. "You have lots of ability you have yet to use, and I want to give you every opportunity to use that potential."

At this point, Bob decided to offer to help Faith advance in her job. Toward that end, he promised to put her in charge of several projects of her own, assignments that would make her more promotable in the future. "If you take these on, I'll be free to work on other tasks," he said, looking at the papers stacked on his visitor's chair. "I'll help you if you run into any difficulties," he promised.

Faith was delighted with the offer. She had left her previous employer because she hadn't felt appreciated. Bob clearly recognized her potential and was willing to help her realize it. Bob didn't formalize his promise in a written agreement because he didn't see this as a formal relationship. He'd help her and she, in turn, would help him. That was all there was to his offer.

Bob identified a number of the skills Faith would need to develop the ability to handle the projects and ultimately to become a buyer or an assistant purchasing manager. These included how to use cost and price analysis techniques to rationalize the total cost of acquisition strategies and how to resolve common problems in negotiating contract terms and conditions, and what red flags to look for in contracts and supplier agreements.

Bob promised Faith that he would meet with her every second week in his office at lunchtime—he'd pick up the sandwiches at a nearby deli himself—and that at each meeting she could give him an update on her progress on the projects he would assign, and he would offer her feedback as well as any advice he might have based on his experience with the people Faith would be working with.

In examining what happened, it's important to note two things. First, and foremost, Bob never promised Faith a promotion. As her manager, it would have been a violation of corporate policy to do so. As a mentor of a direct report, you can only offer to help the individual increase his or her employability. Given the volatility of today's workplace, realistically that is all you can offer, anyway.

Equally interesting, as is usually the case at the start of mentoring relationships, the word *mentor* never came up. Indeed, the term wasn't used until two years later, when Faith's husband had to relocate and Faith therefore left the company.

THE FRUITS OF AN EXCELLENT MENTORING RELATIONSHIP

Faith's daughter Raquel came to the office on her mother's last day there, and she was introduced to "Bob Andrews, my boss and mentor." Faith's husband wasn't the only person with a new job in the new city; Faith had one, too. Through Bob's network of contacts, she had landed a job in which she would be assistant manager of purchasing in her new location. Her experience had built up her self-confidence to the point that she had no trepidation about her new career move.

The use of the word *mentor* had surprised Bob; he had seen the relationship more as a partnership: In return for the free time he gained from Faith's assuming projects he would otherwise have had to oversee himself, he helped Faith with advice about the assignments he had given her and also recommended opportunities for training that would move her out of her current job track. But in retrospect, he had to agree that he had been her mentor. He had taught her a lot and advised her on the training she would need to get the new job. But it had been a win/win/win arrangement. Faith had developed the skills she needed to succeed in her new job, but in the process she had also uncovered a vendor scam that would have cost Bob's and Faith's organization more than $50,000. She had learned about the ruse during one of the evening courses she had taken. Bob's boss had nominated her for an individual achievement certificate, which she received along with the $5,000 bonus that went with it.

Bob hadn't done poorly either. Freed of the more mundane projects he had responsibility for, he had been able to complete a reorganization plan for the purchasing department, thereby saving the company another $100,000. His reward from the company had been an upgrading and a salary increase.

How a Mentoring Relationship Succeeds

What made Faith and Bob's mentoring relationship work so well? To answer that question, we have to consider the two individuals. Looking at what Faith brought to the relationship will give you some idea of the kinds of staff or team members who can get the most benefit from mentoring.

FATIH'S PROMISING BACKGROUND

Faith had a track record that showed she was willing to assume responsibility for her own growth and development. Raquel was three years old when Faith had returned to college to complete her studies toward a bachelor's degree in English. With no real job skills, she had entered the job market as a receptionist while attending business school to learn the latest software programs, accounting and business law, and office management. She had gone to secretarial school and then entered the workforce because of the family's need for a second income, but she had wanted to continue school and get a master's degree in business administration, she had admitted to Bob.

With some careful probing, Bob discovered that Faith's father had been against her attending college right after high school. Her decision to return to school when Raquel was three had upset her parents, who felt that she should be sufficiently happy as a housewife and mother. Her husband supported her decision, but Faith's parents tried to discourage her, pointing to the damage it might do to her marriage and relationship with her young daughter. Although she made light of it, their lack of support had made her less confident about her decision—and any future endeavors. Still, her job record demonstrated that she thrived on challenges.

A Dynamic Career

In her first job, as a receptionist, she had done the clerical tasks for the head of office services while manning the outer desk. Because the manager had seen how knowledgeable Faith was about a new software program the firm had installed, she had asked Faith to give an overview of the program to the firm's secretaries, and Faith had put together a training program and followed it up by instituting a user's group within the company. If there had been a position as secretary available for Faith, she would have been given it, the office manager had told Bob when he did a reference check on Faith. "We just didn't have the budget to create the position, and there was no likelihood of a vacancy in the near future."

Faith's first secretarial job was with a marketing manager. Soon after starting, she was not only opening his correspondence but writing much of it, as well as completing market research reports under his direction. And so it went.

Faith had worked as secretary for two companies before being hired by Bob. In each instance, she had actively sought challenging assignments and taken on greater responsibilities. She was continually learning because she accepted feedback and coaching well, learning from those who were willing to share their know-how with her.

An Eye on Self-Development

Bob was particularly impressed by Faith's participation in their discussions about her developmental needs. On her own, she contacted several local universities to get course catalogues, and then she reviewed their contents with Bob to determine which courses would most help her become more familiar with her department's responsibilities. While attending a course, she would ask Bob question about what she was learning to better understand its application to their department.

In summary, Bob recognized Faith's abilities and she, in turn, was willing to take on additional responsibilities in return for his helping her to advance in her career. She knew she would have to assume more work than her peers, but she recognized that her relationship with Bob would work only if it benefited him and the organization as well as her. She used her semi-monthly meetings to increase her employability and ability to complete Bob's assignments. While Bob had agreed to help her, Faith knew that she was still responsible for her own development and she took the initiative in working with him to meet her developmental goals.

All wasn't rosy with Faith's performance. On two occasions, she failed to complete projects on schedule, and Bob was annoyed, although he tried not to show it as he explained to her that she would have to learn to balance her time. Yes, he understood that she had a home life as well as her new studies and job responsibilities, but he gently reminded her about the developmental plan.

He suggested that she talk over some of her home tasks with her husband to see if he would lend a hand when she had a critical office deadline.

Faith followed Bob's advice, and found her husband entirely supportive of her career advancement goals.

Most important, Faith recognized the importance of mutual respect, trust, and openness. Which is why Bob learned about Faith's need to relocate immediately after the family decision was made. She could have waited at least two months to let him know, but she didn't, and thereby risked not going on her first business trip as a representative of the firm. Bob appreciated the advance notice, and was able to get approval for replacements—yes, he discovered that he would need two to replace Faith—and, in return for her openness, he sent her and one of the department's buyers on the trip as planned.

The Characteristics of an Excellent Mentee

What made Faith such a good mentee? The answer is multifaceted but clear:

◇ *She had a track record of success.*

◇ *She had demonstrated her intelligence and initiative in previous jobs.*

◇ *She was loyal to the organization and committed to its values.*

◇ *She shared with Bob a desire to achieve results.*

◇ *She enjoyed challenges and willingly accepted greater responsibility.*

◇ *She took responsibility for her own career advancement and growth.* To this end, she planned the action steps that would lead to achievement of her career goals.

◇ *She valued feedback even if it wasn't always positive.* She realized that she could make mistakes, but rarely did she repeat them because she listened to and followed the advice more experienced individuals gave her.

◇ *She welcomed Bob's help in identifying her performance deficiencies and setting developmental goals.*

The Characteristics of an Excellent Mentor

What about Bob? What made him such a good mentor?

◇ *He had strong interpersonal skills.* Although Bob liked to work with numbers, which is why he chose to work in the purchasing field, he also liked working with people. And he had good communication skills, which means he was not only articulate but an active listener. A practitioner of the 20/80 rule, he listened 80 percent of the time and talked only 20 percent in most communications with his staff members. He knew how to ask open-ended questions—that is, questions that require more than yes or no answers—and he listened to the responses, nodding and moving toward the speaker in a manner that demonstrated he wanted to hear more.

He often paraphrased what he had been told to ensure that he understood what the other party said.

Rather than answer all Faith's questions, Bob also found it worthwhile to ask her more questions to force her to think through situations and come up with the right answers herself.

◇ *He had contacts both within and outside the organization, and tremendous influence within the company.* Bob shared with Faith the insights about the company's long-range goals and strategic intent he had gained from the movers and shakers within the organization. This knowledge allowed her to identify those who might be obstacles to completing the projects assigned her and to develop plans to gain these individuals' support. Consequently she was able to develop an impressive track record that was attracting the attention of senior management. Clearly, with access to Bob's extensive network of resources, Faith was positioned to apply for the next assistant managerial position that opened up within the organization. And she would have been made an assistant manager had she not had to relocate.

Still, Bob's contacts in the field meant that she was able to get a comparable job in purchasing in a company in her new location.

◇ *He recognized others' accomplishments.* Bob had learned how motivating this could be. So he went out of his way to acknowledge the accomplishments of those with whom he worked.

He never took credit for the work of his employees. But neither did he praise them unless it was deserved—because he understood that praise that is not legitimately earned has little or no value; it even undermines the value of the giver.

◇ *He was an excellent supervisor.* That he is able to give feedback that clearly reinforces the desired performance and to coach to improve performance makes Bob not only an excellent manager but also an excellent mentor. He knows how to delegate tasks, determine adequate time for completion of the task, communicate clearly what needs to be done, estimate resource requirements and see that they are forthcoming. . . . The list goes on, but the bottom line is that a good mentor is someone who manages people successfully.

◇ *He knows his field.* Since Bob's competence in purchasing is acknowledged by those in his organization, his recognition of Faith's accomplishments carried weight. Bob maintains his expertise through his attendance at local and annual meetings of associations in his field and industry.

Since he has spoken at several industry conferences, his prestige extends beyond the boundaries of his organization, which gives him leverage both within and outside the company—leverage that he can use to help a mentee.

◇ *He accepts the risk that comes with mentoring.* There is no guarantee that each time a mentee steps outside her box she will be successful. A mentor has to have the courage to know that the person he is sponsoring may sometimes fail and to be willing to be there to support that person should she be beyond her depths. A mentor is someone who says enthusiastically to the mentee "Go to it!" but who also is prudent about the risks he lets the employee take on. After all, the mentor wants the mentee not only to build new skills but also to increase her self-confidence from a stream of wins.

◇ *He is willing to be available to help another advance in the organization.* Bob was willing to commit both his time and his emotional energy to Faith because he felt she was worth the effort. He wasn't threatened by the thought that one day Faith might even surpass him. He realized he could move her career forward by sharing with her the "unwritten rules" about the organization, wisdom he had gained the hard way from breaking the rules himself. But if he hadn't, Faith could easily have been a bull in a china shop in trying to complete the projects Bob assigned her.

During his meetings, Bob also had to listen to her insecurities and help her answer "What if . . ." questions. He had to let her test ideas, listen to them objectively, advise on the wisdom of pursuing them, help Faith adapt them as appropriate, and then help Faith to present the idea to others in the best light.

In short, he had to be willing to devote time to Faith's career— two hours every two weeks or four hours a month. More than this would have been too much, making Faith overdependent on Bob. On the other hand, even four hours, given the time pressures on most managers, represent a major commitment. After all, four hours are the equivalent of one team meeting or two vendor interviews, or two lunches with his own boss, or a review of a stack of requisitions. Regardless, it was a commitment Bob had to keep.

Consider what might have happened if he had not kept his promise to meet with Faith regularly over lunch to discuss her progress, even if he had had legitimate reasons for not being available. It's likely it would have done just the opposite of what he intended: His superstar's performance would have faded.

Your Prospective Mentoring Relationship

Let's look at that high-value employee you identified. How successful will you be in mentoring this person? To measure the likelihood of success of your entering into a mentorship, on a sheet of paper list in one column the resources (skills, abilities, knowledge) you are willing to give to the relationship, including your commitment of time and attention. In the other column, list your prospective mentee's needs. Now review the two lists.

Begin with your prospective mentee's list. First check those occasions for spur-of-the-moment interventions like a review by you of the mentee's proposal, prior to his presenting it to the team, to help the talented but inexperienced public speaker identify any trouble spots. The items remaining would be those developmental needs that demand a greater commitment from you. For instance, maybe the employee mentee has great ideas but can't sell them and needs someone to provide ongoing coaching to enable him to stand out from the team.

Now look at your own list of skills, abilities, and knowledge, including political know-how, that you can use to assist your mentee. Draw lines across the two columns where you can link your competencies very specifically with the employee mentee's developmental needs. Use a yellow marker to note those instances in which the mentee might be better off with another mentor, either because the need demands more time than you are able to give or because you lack skill in that area.

Now examine the two lists as well as the number of yellow marks on the finished sheet of paper. Needless to say, the more yellow marks, there are, the less likely it is that the mentorship will help the mentee, and the more frustrated both you and the mentee will be from getting together for talks that produce no real return.

The more linkages there are between your mentee's needs and your resources, the more productive the mentorship will be. Even if the mentee has a high need for help, so long as you have sufficient time and skills to satisfy the individual's developmental needs, the relationship should work well for both of you.

And assuming that you have entered into the relationship with a clear idea of its benefits to you—from reducing the learning curve of a new hire to making a talented employee into an informal assistant or project leader, to keeping a champion in top form—there should be every reason for you to commit yourself to this person's professional and personal development.

One caveat: Be honest about the time you can commit to the individual. We all have a tendency to underestimate the amount of our work and to overestimate the time available. So reduce by at least one-third your estimate of available time to help the mentee employee. While mentoring someone isn't as time-intensive as some people suppose, it should still be obvious that a very needful mentee with an overloaded mentor will not work well together.

Chapter 10

Solving Problems Before They Happen

In Chapter 9 you saw how mentoring can be used to boost the performance of your best performers or help a new hire with lots of ability to hit the ground running. But mentoring can also be used to prevent a decline in performance from these same employees. Recognizing how mentoring can be used to keep top performers at their current high levels—and to keep them from deserting the company—is as germane to this section of the book as is how to use it to motivate your best employees to do even more.

Reaping Unexpected Benefits

When Eric decided to assume the role of Maria's mentor, he expected good things to result for Maria, himself, his engineering department, and the company. But he never expected the mentoring relationship to bring about a cultural change for the better in his department.

HOW MENTORING CHANGED A CORPORATE CULTURE

Maria was one of Erik's best performers. She always came up with great ideas for improving the firm's line of electronic components or less expensive ways of producing them. Since the market was undergoing one of its shifts, and dollars were short and sales down, Maria's creativity was an asset. It was an asset that Erik had begun to worry about losing.

Maria had come up with a system improvement, but management had turned down her suggestion because of the short-term costs. The company would have to pay the costs of terminating a contract with a supplier and change several plant processes, but over the long term the new components would be cheaper to produce. There was also a ready market for the new components.

Erik had heard that Maria was so disappointed about having her idea rejected that she had begun to talk about leaving the firm for a company that could see beyond the first or second quarter. Although neither Erik nor Maria had ever used the word *mentor* during their once-a-month lunches, Erik had assumed that role with his superstar. And Erik felt that he should do more than merely commiserate with her, particularly if he didn't want to lose her to the competition.

Laying a Reputation on the Line

Consequently, he prepared a memo for his boss and others in senior management in favor of Maria's proposal, putting his ten years in the industry on her side. A patent holder many times over, Erik was known both for his creativity and for the ability to implement his ideas. He put that reputation on the line for Maria. And he got management's approval for her idea.

It worked. Management took the financial hurt during the first two quarters, but once the new component was on the retuned production line, the numbers quickly turned around. Costs declined 15 percent while sales jumped almost 30 percent. And Maria was so delighted with her bonus that she confided to Erik that she had no desire to leave. Besides, she had other ideas for further perfecting the line that she wanted to try.

But there is more to the story than Erik acting as advocate for his mentee. His support of Maria had an effect throughout the engineering department. Morale rose as the news of what Erik had done spread. The engineers began to come to Erik with ideas that they had developed but had never shared with him before. Erik found himself mentoring more than Maria when he discovered several potential superstars on his team as these former mediocre performers found that their creativity would be recognized.

Erik's engineering group became the benchmark for innovation in the industry. There also was a decline in turnover.

As the engineers learned that Erik had put his own job on the line for one of his engineers, and saw that he was willing to go above and beyond his responsibility as their manager to help his employees, employee loyalty lost as the result of a deep downsizing about a year before returned—not to the organization but to Erik.

Averting Problems Through Mentoring

To bring home the benefits of mentoring in terms of individual effectiveness, let me share with you two other stories—about Mike Ford and Julio Perez.

Sandy, Mike, and Julio

Both Mike and Julio reported to Sandy Lester, head of the marketing division for Acme Assets, a California-based financial services firm, and both were marketing managers at this time. Julio had been with the company for only a little over a month, whereas Mike had been there for three years. Mike was overdue for promotion, but there was nowhere within the organization he could go.

Both men were excellent workers, but it wasn't their current performance that was Sandy's concern but whether they would continue to produce at their current high levels. They both represented problems on the verge of happening if Sandy didn't avert them—through mentoring.

Julio asked to meet with Sandy to find out if he had made the right decision in leaving his previous employer to take a job with Acme.

Since he had joined the company, Julio had heard rumblings from his colleagues about the likelihood of a downsizing. Julio's decision had been financially beneficial, but he had not known about two downsizings in other areas of the organization; he was concerned that the rumors might be true and that there would be cuts in marketing and he might be one of the first to be let go. As one of his new peers reminded him over lunch, "Last hired, first fired."

Julio was also concerned because he might not be able to do his job well if the company was tightfisted about the money it laid out for marketing efforts. Consequently, besides making an appointment to meet with Sandy to discuss the situation later in the day, Julio also tried to reach his boss at his old company to see if his job there was still open, just in case.

Mike had an appointment with Sandy to talk about his plateaued status. He also wanted to find out if it was true what he had heard from a friend in Human Resources: Julio was making $10,000 more a year than he was. Mike, one of Sandy's stars, was hurting because he had thought his work was respected. That a new hire might make more than he did made him wonder if he really should be putting in all those long hours and weekends. Mike was being courted by one of Acme's competitors, and until now he had rejected their overtures. But he was considering visiting with the company's marketing VP to discuss the offer.

Sandy found herself in the position of possibly losing two of her best performers in one and the same day if she didn't come up with acceptable answers to their career concerns. She suspected that Mike was frustrated about his promotion prospects, but she had no idea what was troubling Julio. Since they were her two top performers, she was concerned about the impact their declining morale would have not only on their own work but on the performance of the team as a whole.

Julio's Meeting

A very direct person, Julio got to the point of the meeting immediately: Why hadn't Sandy mentioned that there had been layoffs before he was hired? Sandy was taken aback. "Yes," she said, "there have been downsizings within the organization, but none have occurred within this operation. Actually, this division has been given approval to hire because it is launching two new products in the coming year." One of these products had been assigned to Julio; the other had gone to Mike.

Further, because the company had high hopes for both products, Sandy told Julio, he had "no reason to be concerned that the budget would be cut. There had been some objections raised to the marketing campaign, but its cost certainly wasn't an issue," she continued.

As Sandy fielded each of Julio's questions, she realized that he had been listening to the wrong people. She had thought Julio was experienced enough to be able to steer his own way through his new company's political byways, but judging from his comments he clearly wasn't. It looked as if he needed her help to separate the truth from the rumors and to identify whom to trust and whom not to trust. Since it was likely he would encounter some small opposition to his marketing plans for the new product, it was certainly worthwhile for her to serve as his adviser and broker until he had gained the respect his past job history suggested he deserved.

Sandy answered each of Julio's concerns, and as she did so, she noticed the muscles around his mouth ease and his body relax into the chair.

"I'm sorry," Julio stammered. "I guess I was jumping to lots of conclusions. Next time, I'll talk to you before losing my head."

"Yes, please," said Sandy. Then, after thinking for a minute, she suggested that she and Julio meet over lunch once a week for the next few weeks while he better familiarized himself with the operation. "I can help you through some of the traps you could encounter working with the product managers here," she said. "Besides, we have just installed several new systems. Even our old-timers are having a hard time adapting. I'd like to see that you get off on the right foot."

Julio was flattered. At his previous company, he had had to find his own way around during his first few weeks. But his new boss here was offering to help him over the political obstacles and to give him any support he might need to get his new marketing campaign off the ground.

Sandy told Julio to ask her assistant to schedule lunch with Julio every Wednesday for the next two months, and Julio promised to be ready to show Sandy the design for the new product's campaign over lunch in two days. He then scurried back to his office to schedule meetings with a designer and copywriter.

"One problem down," thought Sandy. "I hope I can be as successful with Mike. He's usually so upbeat and enthusiastic, but lately he has been sullen, glaring at me if not avoiding me entirely."

Mike's Complaint

When Mike entered Sandy's office, he looked almost in pain. His humorous manner and twinkling eyes had made meetings with him over the past three years pleasurable, but Sandy seemed unable to get even a smile from him now. "Are you angry?" she finally asked.

"Yes, I'm angry," he said, clenching his teeth so the words barely came out.

"About what?" Sandy asked, trying to defuse the situation by making light of it. When Mike only grimaced, Sandy realized she had to change her tactics. She quietly moved her chair from behind the desk so that she was sitting at right angles to Mike. "Tell me what's bothering you," she asked.

"It's everything. I know that we have had only one opening in the division and it was a lateral—at least, I thought it was until I heard about Julio's salary."

"Oh," said Sandy.

"Yes," said Mike, gaining courage. "I hear he's making at least $10,000 more than any of us. I've been here three years, and am long overdue for a promotion. Why didn't you offer me the position?"

"It was posted," Sandy said defensively, then calmed herself. "But it is the same grade as yours. Julio's salary is only slightly higher than yours—certainly not $10,000 more—and he is getting what he is getting because that's what the market demands. You know all about compressed salaries and the like," she added.

"Yes, sure, but how come he is being put in charge of our newest financial offering?" he continued, still upset.

"We have two products that senior management has targeted for major marketing campaigns," Sandy explained. "Although Julio is new to the firm, he's familiar with the targeted market, so I gave him one. I gave you the other. Both are so important that it would have been unwise to assign both to a single marketer," Sandy said.

"Sandy," Mike complained, "I don't know. Maybe I shouldn't be as upset as I am, but I've been in the same position now for three years. I'm good—really good at what I do— and yet we both know there is nowhere in this office right now for me to advance to."

Sandy's Reply

When Mike finished his lament, Sandy admitted that all of what he said was true. She then said, "I haven't really shown you how important you are to our operation, have I?

"You're right that, since our delayering of the organization, there is no opportunity for advancement for you right now," Sandy continued. "But there are a number of critical assignments you could take over that would tell others within the organization how highly regarded you are. Would you be willing to take over one or more of these? These are projects I have been asked to spearhead, but if you are willing, I'd be delighted to have you handle one yourself and work with me on another. What do you say?"

"There wouldn't be a raise in this, would there?" Mike asked.

"No, I can't promise that. But if you do a good job, it will certainly be reflected in your performance appraisal and the regard with which others in the company and industry hold you. In fact, you'll likely have people within the company knocking down your door to get you to help with projects of their own—and I don't even want to think about how involvement in these projects will increase other companies' interest in you."

Suddenly Mike smiled. "I like working for you, Sandy. Money isn't really as important to me as knowing that my work is appreciated," he said. Sandy knew Mike well enough to know that he was telling the truth.

"Tomorrow is Tuesday," Sandy said, thinking out loud, "let's arrange to get together after 4:00 p.m. so we can discuss the two projects. Let Marie know," she said.

"I may need to meet with you during the project to ensure that everything goes well," Mike said as he headed for the door.

"Of course. After I've explained the projects to you tomorrow, we can decide on how frequently we need to get together to monitor project progress. And, Mike," Sandy added, "if you ever again have doubts about how important you are to this organization, please put them aside. You have some of the most creative ideas in the department; even P. T. Barnum couldn't have come up with such audience-grabbing ideas."

As Sandy readjusted her chair behind her desk, she signaled Marie at her desk. "Marie," she said, "note on my calendar that I should ask Mike out for lunch in about two weeks. I'm putting him in charge of Project Phantom, and he'll need me to advise him on how to get through the political minefield so that he gets all the resources he'll need."

As she leaned back at her desk, Sandy thought about the afternoon. Not only had she stopped two performance problems from occurring but she had motivated two of her top workers, and very likely she would see even greater performance from both in the future. "I'm a darn good coach," Sandy thought, making the mistake of many managers in confusing mentoring with coaching.

Summing Up

In essence, Sandy was offering to mentor Julio's orientation in the organization when she offered to help him become comfortable with the firm's new systems and to guide him with the political issues he might face in getting his new marketing campaign off the ground. That included acting as a broker to ensure that he had the resources he would need to make his ideas a success.

Whereas Sandy needed to mentor Julio for only a few weeks, she had to spend longer with Mike, providing a sounding board as he learned new project management skills under her direction, skills that had nothing to do with his current job. With both Julio and Mike—but for different reasons—Sandy had to provide sketches of both the organization and its members, providing information that the new mentees ordinarily would not have been privy to or been able easily to discover on their own.

During her later meetings with Julio and Mike, Sandy answered lots of questions, but more important were the questions she asked to help her new mentees develop personal and professional insights. The questions were thought-provoking, prompting her mentee employees to begin thinking about the kinds of situations or issues that might arise and how they would handle them. If they didn't have the skills they needed, the questions were designed to prompt them to ask Sandy about future developmental efforts.

Mentoring can be a preventive of performance problems and

an effective tool in performance management, but only if the mentor is skillful in getting a dialogue going with the mentee.

How to Generate Discussion

Interestingly, the secret to getting a productive mentoring discussion going is not to begin with a question but rather with a statement that tells the mentee the direction in which the discussion will go. The mentor's opening statement tells the mentee what page the mentor is on; it also spotlights the issue that will be discussed. For instance:

In Sandy's meeting with Mike at 4:00 p.m. on Tuesday, she began with a statement that focused the subsequent discussion on one of the political issues that Mike would have to address to complete Project Phantom on schedule.

Sandy: Mike, you have worked with Tim Gilmour?
Mike: Yes, I've been on some teams with him recently. When I first came here, I had to lend a hand when his marketing manager took maternity leave.
Sandy: What have you learned about how he works?
Mike: He is very numbers-oriented.
Sandy: How did the numbers he demanded differ from those that Larry Nichols regularly asks for in connection with marketing his product line?''

Sandy was encouraging Mike to compare work styles so as to help him work successfully with Tim on the Phantom Project. But she was far from through.

She had to continue to probe to be sure that Mike saw specifically why Gilmour operated as he did ("How is Tim cost-conscious?") and that Mike appreciated how he would have to adapt his own work style to work effectively with Gilmour ("When you work with Tim, what will you be doing differently from the way you currently work?").

Throughout that first meeting, she used statements followed by provocative questions to get Mike to develop an action plan for handling his new project:

Sandy: You did a good job introducing our new mutual fund offer, but you'll need to move more quickly with Project Phantom. The CEO understands it is your first time heading up a project.
Mike: Will Gilmour help me?
Sandy: Would you feel comfortable asking him?
Mike: I think so. Do you have some suggestions for how to introduce the topic?
Sandy: You've worked with Tim before.
Mike: Yes. He likes being asked for help.
Sandy: How would you ask him to co-lead the project?

And so that meeting and subsequent meetings went.

Few of the questions that Sandy raised in her first meeting and in subsequent sessions began with "why" because "why" questions seem to put people on the defensive, making them feel as if they have to justify their actions. Sandy wanted to encourage an open discussion, and she knew that "why" questions might have put either Julio or Mike in a guarded frame of mind.

Advice vs. Feedback

Although mentors act as advisers to their protégés, they should more often provide feedback than advice. Unsolicited advice only draws resentment, whereas feedback, when offered correctly, instructs the person getting the feedback. A secret to getting someone to *really* listen to the feedback you are offering—and helpful in any mentoring situation—is to make clear to the mentee that he or she would have discovered and addressed the problem without your help. Your purpose in offering the feedback is to speed the developmental process.

As you give feedback during mentoring, remember the advice I gave in connection with coaching: Give the feedback in a straightforward and honest manner. Ask yourself how you would like someone to assess something you have done. Very likely, you would want that feedback to be clear but empathetic. You wouldn't want to be told something in a cruel or hypercritical manner.

On the other hand, you don't want to feel that the person responsible for giving you feedback is holding back. You want to feel that you can trust this person not to wimp out because he or she is uncomfortable with being open or honest with you.

In many ways, a mentorship is a form of friendship. Consider how you would give advice to a close friend:

Claire, a manager, recently told me about a situation in which a friend of hers was involved. The friend had been passed over for a promotion, and Claire's friend wanted to complain to Human Resources about the failure of her boss to give her the promotion.

"My friend was furious. She felt a principle was involved."

As Claire explained it to me, her friend had applied for a job in a company that claimed that internal candidates would get first consideration; yet her friend had learned that her boss had already interviewed several external candidates before meeting with inside applicants. Further, the boss had not noted all the requirements for the job, and while Claire's friend met these requirements as well, she had focused only on those in the posted notice.

Claire's friend wanted to report her boss to Human Resources and even to senior management. Yet she still worked for this individual and had no prospects for a job outside!

"Yes, it was unfair," Claire told me. "But my friend Taylor had to be made to realize that going to Human Resources in her present mood would do her no good."

Interestingly, Claire did exactly as Sandy had with Julio and Mike. She asked her friend questions both to calm her and to get her to consider her various options and the consequences of each. Ultimately, Claire's friend went to her boss and discussed what had happened, but she decided to wait several days until she had calmed herself.

Claire didn't tell her friend what to do; she didn't even tell her what she would do in a similar situation. Rather, she asked gently probing questions that helped her friend find a way to address the "principle" without alienating her boss.

To measure your communication skills as a mentor, ask yourself the following questions. The more often you can answer no to them, the better able you are to mentor one of your employees to increased individual effectiveness:

◇ Do you jump in with solutions before you have heard out your employee about a problem he or she is having?
◇ Do you believe there is only one way to handle a situation?
◇ Do you remain calm even when someone in whom you had faith lets you down?
◇ Do you get visibly annoyed when you have to go over the same issue time and again until the individual with whom you are speaking understands why the subject is important?
◇ Do you tell people what to do rather than lead them by asking thought-provoking questions?
◇ Do you have a reputation for avoiding awkward conversations or addressing sensitive issues?
◇ Even though you can't guarantee it, do you make promises to staff members about getting them a promotion or giving them a bonus if they do such and such?
◇ Do you allow others to interrupt while you are meeting with employees about their career concerns?
◇ Do you lie occasionally about the realities of career advancement in your organization and recommend unrealistic paths to advancement to avoid addressing the limited opportunities available?
◇ Do you throw individuals into the water of new experiences without being present to throw them a lifesaver?
◇ Do you gab over lunch with colleagues about the weaknesses of your employees?

What Sandy Did for Julio and Mike

You may be wondering what happened to the marketing managers Julio and Mike, who worked for Sandy at Acme Assets. Actually, all three stories have a happy ending.

THREE SUCCESS STORIES

Julio remained as marketing manager with Acme for four years and ultimately moved up to take Sandy's job when she was promoted to senior management. On the other hand, Mike, despite his close ties to Acme, ultimately left two years after his meeting with Sandy, but they were two years of tremendous success for him and the company—and for Sandy. Why do you think she advanced to senior management?

Sandy's friendship with Mike continued after he left, so she was delighted to find Mike at her promotion party. At that meeting, Mike listed the many reasons why he enjoyed working with Sandy. Interestingly, several reflected her mentoring style more than they did her managerial style. For instance, Sandy:

◇ *Allowed him the freedom to do things his own way.* Mike noted how Sandy recognized when he needed help to advance in his career, but she didn't let him become dependent on her by doing all the thinking for him. Rather, she asked him questions that made him think. The projects she gave him were within his reach, but they also required him to stretch.

"Yes, she had solutions that she could offer. But," Mike said, "she led me through a thinking process to help me choose how best *I* should handle the situation. Sandy can be very explicit when she knows you are confused about what to do next, and you seek her out for direction," he told the group. "But she also encouraged me to try new approaches to a situation. Sandy made me aware of the various paths I could take to achieve a goal, but she let me choose my own routes."

◇ *Gave him a developmental plan with individual goals to aim for.* Mike told the assembled group how he and Sandy had set goals for him that would make him a more skilled project manager. "I looked back on those goals," he said, "and I discovered something. Each one was designed to move me forward—each small win built my confidence and prepared me to achieve my next goal. The developmental plan we created," Mike observed, "built on my strengths as well as addressed my development needs."

◇ *Acknowledged she wasn't perfect.* "I knew I was going to make mistakes leading the projects I handled," he told the assembled group, "but I was surprised when Sandy admitted to mistakes she had made during the first times she headed up a project."

Employee mentees need to know that their mentor made errors along the way as well as to hear about the mentor's accomplishments. This prepares the mentee for the problems he might encounter while pursuing a goal. Parenthetically, it also makes a mentee (or, for that matter, someone being coached or counseled) more receptive to negative feedback; after all, in most instances, the person offering the feedback gained her wisdom the hard way.

◇ *Always followed up on tasks assigned others.* "Sandy followed up as she promised," Mike observed. Too often a mentor will give an employee a project and then fail to monitor his work to see if he completes the assignment or to ask about the nature of the problems he is having. Some mentors don't want to follow up because they are afraid they will find problems, which will put them in the unenviable position of having to criticize the mentee. But the reality is that problems can arise, and a mentor isn't doing her job if she doesn't raise these issues.

Everything Mike said ties in closely with the most important elements in a mentoring relationship: trust and mutual respect. These are the foundation stones of a successful mentorship. The mentee has to trust the mentor to keep their conversations confidential and to be honest about any problems either in the relationship itself or in the mentee's work. And both mentor and mentee must respect each other and be able to carry on open communications with one another without concern about hurting the other party's feelings.

Chapter 11

Team Sponsorship

Besides mentoring your best employees, you can also mentor a group of outstanding employees working as a team, either a self-directed team or a cross-functional group. In this context, you would likely be called a "sponsor" rather than a "mentor," although you would perform all the roles of a mentor, from role model to adviser, to broker, to advocate.

You may also mentor teams that were not formed to make your own ideas a reality. Sometimes, you may be asked by your boss or another member of senior management to put together a team to handle a project. You aren't the team's leader—actually, you aren't a member of the team at all—but, as team sponsor, you play a major role in all four stages of team management: forming, storming, norming, and performing.

The Forming Stage of Team Management

In the first stage, the team is assembled and its mission is formalized. As team mentor, you have the following five responsibilities.

Saying Yay or Nay to a Team

You shouldn't fall into the trap of many managers and form a team to pursue an idea before you have thought about how best to accomplish the mission. Teams are a very popular way to get things done today, but they aren't always the most efficient or most effective way to accomplish something. There may be another option for achieving the objective, particularly if you are mentoring an exceptional employee with both the skills to handle the project on his own and the desire to take on the assignment in order to advance his career.

The mentee can accomplish the same goal as a team if it's to get information from others, for instance. The information gathering can be handled by telephone or through e-mail or by a one-on-one meeting in the office or over coffee and bagels at breakfast or burgers at lunch. It's even possible today to get a group together on a corporate intranet for a one-time exchange of information to solve a problem or to get information to make a decision. The decision and implementation of that idea may not demand a group effort.

Remember, a good mentor is a good manager. Good managers know when to use a team. My earlier book *The High-Value Manager: Developing the Core Competencies Your Organization Demands*, coauthored with Randi T. Sachs, notes that "high-value managers"—that is, managers who are valued by their organizations because they bring the right skills, ability, and knowledge to situations—create teams only when the individuals can bring together a variety of perspectives that will contribute to a better idea and when integration of different kinds of knowledge and skills can both open networks of information not available to a single manager and increase acceptance and therefore successful implementation of the final idea.

Determining Team Structure

Should you decide you need a team to accomplish your objective, your next step is to consider how best to organize that team. Do you want to bring together the best individuals from throughout the organization or to form a team made up solely of your own top employees? Do you think the team's mission will require a large group or a small one, a group led by your appointee or a self-directed work team?

Identifying Prospective Team Members

Let's assume that you decide you will need a cross-functional team. The individuals you select ideally should have strong interpersonal skills, but that is of secondary consideration to knowledge in their functional area if the project has a strong technical bias. If the project's mission calls for a major change in organizational strategy or direction, you should also review your list of candidates to determine which of those individuals are unafraid of change; you don't want those with caretaker mentalities.

You may think you know already whom you want for your team, but to be sure that you have all the expertise you will need, you may want to use a skills inventory matrix (see table) to ensure that you identify all the competencies you require and those on staff with such abilities, skills, or knowledge.

Team Member Matrix/Business Plan						
	Hector	Marge	Carole	Jim	Chang	Jackie
Market knowledge		X			X	
Researching capability			X			
Writing skills	X					X
Organization talent				X	X	
Networking	X	X			X	
Technical knowledge			X			

A skills inventory matrix lists on the left side the talents or know-how you will need for the team and on the top the names of staff members who could bring these to the team effort.

Not until you determine which competencies will be important to the team's success should you give thought to deciding who the team members will be.

Consider both those within and outside your department or division. To be sure that you choose the very best candidates, thumb through your company's telephone directory. You wouldn't want to overlook someone who could be a key player in the initiative.

When forming a group, managers first consider those who generally take center stage in everything in which they involve themselves, thereby overlooking those who are equally knowledgeable, if not more so than their more boastful colleagues, have an equally impressive track record, and have more time than their more visible colleagues because their know-how is less recognized.

List your selection of team candidates on the top of the skills inventory matrix and put checks in those boxes to indicate the competencies these individuals would bring to the effort. If there is someone who can bring expertise in more than one area, indicate this in the appropriate boxes. Their broader know-how may give you some flexibility in forming your team as well as keep the group's size down; ideally, teams should not contain more than seven members.

In selecting the leader of your team, you should look for someone who has the ability to motivate others to perform what needs to be done. Which could mean that your prospective leader must be the kind of person who will be willing to share her authority with team members. You don't want as leader someone who insists on doing things only her way and, in doing so, alienates the group. At the same time, you want as leader an individual who won't compromise the team's goals or objectives to avoid confrontation.

If you have a mentee, you should consider him for the leadership spot; in fact, he may even ask to be point person if it's a high-visibility team. Don't let your mentoring relationship influence your decision, however. You may be mentoring someone who is an exceptional technician but who lacks strong people skills (indeed, that may be the area in which you are mentoring him), and team leadership demands someone with both the functional knowledge and the people skills the team needs.

Once you have identified the members of your cross-functional team, your next step is to get them to become part of the project.

Assembling the Team

To make your ideal team a reality, you will have to convince the individuals you have identified to give time to the project. Depending on their positions within the organization, you may also have to talk to their managers to get approval for their participation in the team effort.

In team management jargon, your peers are the "enablers" (or possibly "disablers") since they can authorize or refuse to authorize the use of any resources critical to the team effort—and that includes the time of "doers," or team members, and "supporters," or those who can help the team with information it might not otherwise have access to. As the team's sponsor, you will have to convince all three to work on your project. And through the life of the team project, you will have to sustain their interest and enthusiasm.

Obviously, it is easier to put together a team to work on an idea that comes from top management. Your peers won't want to seem as if they are obstructing a corporate initiative; even if participation could create workflow problems, they are likely to say yes to a request for a staff member's help and even to serve on the team themselves.

If it's your own project, however, you may have a sales job to do, given the little time today's managers and their staffs have and the birth rate of new teams.

Point to those ways in which the project's completion can help your peers. If there is no mutual benefit, then you may need to engage in some brokering (think "negotiating").

The brokering can be done over coffee or lunch, even standing by the network printer; it's informal negotiations in which you approach the other manager, explain your need for him or her or a staff member to participate in the team, and then wait to see what the manager wants in return for lending you a hand.

Even if you have a good managerial reputation for keeping promises made to other managers and a project that has senior management's okay and that has a good chance of succeeding, the other party still holds all the cards. You need to have done some research, to have considered what you can offer in return for a commitment to the team effort, and to have rehearsed your remarks so that the other manager believes you have something to offer.

Be prepared to compromise to get what you want. Maybe you will have to lend one of your staff members to the manager in return for this manager's approval for one of his staffer's involvement in your project. Or, perhaps, the manager will ask you to be a "supporter," advocating one of his own ideas or advocating the idea in management channels, or helping to move the idea forward by providing needed but not easily available information.

One caveat: Before considering it a done deal, be sure that the individual you have bargained for is sufficiently interested in the project to give adequate time to it. If a prospective member—the manager or one of his workers—doesn't see participation as a worthwhile challenge, go back to your skills inventory matrix to see if you have someone already on the team who can fill this person's spot. Or rethink your team. You want members who are enthusiastic enough about the end result to have the patience to hang in there during the early planning stage of the team effort. Otherwise, you may find yourself in the same situation as Linda.

Linda, head of her consumer company's cereal division, discovered too late how important it was to gain commitment from prospective team members to the team's mission. The team's goal was to research untapped markets for the cereal division's product line. Rose, Linda's mentee, was made head of the team, and on paper the team seemed to have more than enough time—two months—to complete its investigation before the budgets were required.

But timing for the project start-up was terrible. Members of the team were themselves tied up in preliminary planning and number crunching for budget closure.

At first, all Rose had to contend with was tardy attendees. But before long, several members of the team regularly began to miss meetings. Worse, one month into the project, three members—those who had been drafted for the effort by division heads who had bargained for their time in return for Linda's advocacy of a new database, more clerical support, and an ad campaign, respectively,—asked to be excused from the project. The division heads got the new database, more clerical support, and an ad campaign, and Linda was able to find replacements for the former team members, but the marketing managers' forced participation on the team in the beginning lost the project valuable time: The group came up with some profitable opportunities, but it completed its work one week too late to have its recommendations considered in building the budgets.

Linda is now racing around the organization trying to get approval on variances to test the new markets identified by the team.

Reviewing the Mission With the Team

As mentor, once you have assembled the team, you have responsibility for attending its first meeting to communicate to the group both the importance of the project to you and the rest of management and to clarify the mission with the group.

Although you or your chosen team leader may have discussed the mission with the group's members individually, you will want to review once again with the group as a whole its reason for being in existence, the limits of its authority, and the date by which its work must be completed. Think of yourself as the captain of a boat, the team leader as helmsperson, and the team as the boat. You all have to agree on the destination before setting out on a course. Your attendance at the group's meeting will lessen the need for course corrections—and should make them easier on your helmsperson should you be forced to call for course changes during the team process.

It may help the group if from the beginning it has a team charter, that is, a written document that defines your expectations for the team. You alone could write this charter if the team was formed to pursue your own idea; however, if the team is involved in a corporatewide project, then you will want to work with key executives, managers, and others to draft the charter. That way it will communicate accurately not only the rationale for the team and the members' responsibilities but also the criteria the team will use to make effective decisions. For instance, there may be decisions that the team can make by itself, decisions that the team can make only with input from you, and decisions that the team must request from higher authority. There may also be nonnegotiables that the team must know about in advance, like the time it has to come up with its recommendations or the amount of money that can be spent to implement a final decision.

The Storming Phase of Team Management

During the storming phase of a team, conflicts arise as ideas are exchanged and action plans are considered and people develop proprietary feelings either about their suggestions or about the roles they think they should play in the team effort. As mentor, you will be needed for two purposes.

Coaching or Counseling the Team Leader

Whether the team leader is your mentee or not, you may find yourself acting as his mentor, listening to the leader's woes, sharing your own experiences to assure him that such problems at this stage are common, and helping the leader to identify approaches for addressing the interpersonal conflicts that have arisen within the team.

If a leader finds himself beyond his depths, you may want to role model those facilitation techniques that will enable the leader to regain control of the group (see Chapter 7). Your role as team mentor or sponsor isn't either to coach or to counsel the team; that's the role of the group's leader. Your responsibility is to be available to the leader to help him identify how to handle conflicts or other problems that arise.

Should a situation be beyond the leader's ability to handle, reassignment of the current leader and replacement with a more experienced one may be preferable to your personally stepping in. Stepping in would likely only weaken the leader's current position and could even further fractionalize the team as each side tried to win your support.

Redirecting Team Effort

In this second phase, as different thoughts surface about the subject of the discussion, there is always the danger that the team, including its leader, will steer off course. As mentor (think "captain"), you have to be there for course corrections.

As you won't be attending meetings, you must agree with the team about the means by which you will monitor the group's progress. Certainly hold brief meetings periodically with the team's leader. But a simpler way to stay abreast of team progress is to be on the routing list of those receiving the minutes of each meeting. You will then be prepared to raise issues with the leader during your scheduled meetings. Members will also know that you are familiar with team progress when they see you copied on the minutes they receive. That you know the nature *and* quality of their contribution will motivate them to support the team effort as well.

If, from reviewing the minutes or from your discussions with the group leader, you see that the team is moving in a direction that is not a part of its charter, you will need to act. What you do will depend on the nature of the shift in focus and the skills of the group's leader.

Not all shifts are bad. Sometimes the team will discover an opportunity that demands further study, even the need to rewrite the original charter. On the other hand, the team may have lost its direction and have to be reminded of its mission; if in its wandering, the team has exceeded the boundaries originally set, the members have to be alerted to this too.

You should be able to mentor good leaders to handle these course corrections on their own. But you may want to make one of your rare appearances at team meetings if you see an opportunity arising from the team's ramblings or if you believe that a continuation of its current direction not only will waste members' time but could also create turf problems or otherwise be counterproductive to its original purpose.

If the opportunity is related to the original purpose of the team, you may want to form a smaller group within the team to study it further while the team as a whole pursues its original agenda. There is also the possibility that this new avenue may be more worth pursuing than the team's original goal. Then you may want to rewrite the team's original charter to enable the group to pursue, instead, this objective, adding new members to the team if that's called for. However you decide to proceed, you don't want to alienate the team's members by making them feel that they will have no input. Commend the group for its foresight and then discuss with the membership how best to explore the idea; even if you decide that the team, either as a whole or in part, can't pursue the idea, promise to keep the membership informed of results from further study of the idea.

Expect some opposition from a few members who may have proprietary feelings about the new opportunity, but be clear that the team must focus on its initial objective. You may conciliate those who want to examine this new course by offering them an opportunity to do so after this project is completed.

The Norming Phase of Team Management

During the norming stage of team management, the group gets down to business. You want to monitor progress to be sure that the team meets its timetable. So, during this phase, you will continue to meet with the team's leader for progress reports and to review meeting minutes. But you have two other responsibilities during this stage.

Keeping the Group Motivated

Most members are enthusiastic when first asked to be part of a team. They see it as an opportunity to share their ideas, network within the organization, and increase their visibility and, consequently, their promotability. But over time it is easy for team members to lose interest, particularly as they find their participation taking up time that they could be spending on their day-to-day work.

As team mentor, your responsibility is to monitor member enthusiasm and to be sure that it doesn't wane.

Attend a meeting now and then to show the group that you continue to be interested in their efforts. Arrange with the team leader for you to attend a meeting when individual members will be reporting on their progress with assignments so that you can praise the individuals on their efforts. You may also want to have the leader provide you with a form on which members' names are listed along with their individual assignments and due dates. This way, you show your familiarity not only with the project as a whole but with individual efforts. If you bump into a team member, you will be prepared to ask about progress on her assignment, congratulate the member on team progress, and reinforce how important the project is to you, your division, or the company as a whole.

If the team includes individuals from other areas of the organization, you want to keep both them and their bosses interested in the team. You don't want a manager to suddenly pull a staff member off the team because of priorities of his own. Let your peers know about senior management's interest in the team's progress. Let them know, too, when one of their own staff members has made a significant contribution to the team. If they are good managers, they will commend the staff member, which will motivate further effort.

Supporting the Team's Access to Resources and Information

As the team's sponsor, you have to share your network of contacts within the organization and outside to get the group the information it needs to move forward. If the team needs more tangible resources, like additional hands or funds, then you have to demonstrate that you will make an effort to get these, too.

If the idea for the team's project came from senior management, getting extra staff or funds will be easier than if the project only serves your own department's interests. Even if the project idea came originally from on high, though, you will still have to make a strong case for people or money in today's budget-conscious organizations. Working with the team leader, you should prepare your request for additional funds so that it clearly states the results to be achieved.

Here's when that written charter can be extremely helpful, particularly if it was a cooperative effort. Indicate in your request how the team needs these additional funds to achieve its mission. If there is a relationship between the team's charter and the strategic direction of your organization, remind those for whom you are running the project and from whom you are requesting these monies of this fact.

Keep the team's leader and members informed of your progress. Your ability to provide resources for the team will influence member enthusiasm, so be prepared to call in favors or do some more brokering. Each member of the team has a responsibility. Yours is seeing that the team has access to the resources it needs to accomplish its objectives.

To determine how good a broker you are, ask yourself these questions:

◇ *How adaptable am I?* If an alternative offer will get my team what it needs, and it doesn't mean a major sacrifice for me or my division, am I willing to give the other party's offer consideration?

◇ *When I enter into a brokering situation, do I know how far I am willing to bend?*

◇ *Do I do my homework ahead of time?* Do I know the other party's objectives, needs, and resources?

◇ *Do I know how far I can go?* There may be resources needed by the team that are beyond your ability to get. Let the team know what these are. Explaining why may help reduce any demoralizing effect lack of the resources may have on the group.

◇ *How would my reputation stand up if the other party investigated my track record as a negotiator?* Over the years, have you kept your promises to other managers? How about sharing the glory if the team succeeds? If you are known as someone who doesn't hog all the credit, you are more likely to work out a deal with a colleague.

The Performing Stage of Team Management

The performing stage is the final phase of cross-functional team management. At this stage, the group produces its recommendations or implements its idea. If the team project was undertaken for you, you need to review the results, then choose to let the team implement its recommendations or not. If you are mentoring the project for another, however, two other functions are involved.

Analyzing the Group's Work Before Submitting Its Conclusions

Identify any weaknesses in the members' arguments or gaps in their thinking that might prevent the group from getting approval to implement its recommendations.

Just as it's important to team members to make a good impression, it is important for you to do the same. As sponsor or mentor of the team, you are even more responsible for the group's efforts than the team leader, since you were given the project to oversee. Any plan based on your team's work is never good enough until it is as good as you, the team leader, and the team members can make it.

Don't be hypercritical, but also don't be so nurturing that you ignore problems with the team's work in order to maintain the team's momentum through this final stage. Make clear that this final task of the team is to make its plan, already good, even better by searching out its weak points. Help the members by asking the same kinds of questions that senior management might ask of them during the formal presentation of their plan or after top management has read the team's final report. For instance:

◇ *Do we have enough information to make our projected recommendations?*
◇ *Where are we short on supporting documentation?* Are there other sources of information to whom we have not gone? Should we do so before submitting our conclusions?
◇ *How accurate are the data we are presenting?*
◇ *Is the process for change that we are proposing overly complex?* Can we simplify our methodology?
◇ *What could go wrong?* If something went wrong, how costly would it be? How would a problem affect other operations within the organization?
◇ *Have we considered the effect of both internal and external developments?* For instance, could an economic downturn severely affect our plan? Depending on the proposal, get the group to think in terms of environmental issues, market shifts, changes in government regulations, and the like.
◇ *What contingency plans can we offer in the event of either an internal or an external development like those identified?*
◇ *Is there a cheaper way of achieving our recommendations?*
◇ *Must we go outside for the resources we need to implement our plan?* Could we accomplish the same goals internally?

A Problem of Information Accuracy

Barbara ran into a problem over one of the questions in the foregoing list—the accuracy of the information her team would be using in implementing its idea—when she submitted a proposal to senior management to increase sales from existing customers. As head of customer service, she had been looking for a way to increase customer retention, and a mailing campaign suggested by an article in a business magazine had prompted her to form a team to investigate the idea further. The team had come back with further suggestions that, it said, could increase customer retention by 15 percent. The simple mailing campaign in which customers would get reminder notes from field reps had taken a back seat to a major promotional effort in which customers would receive brochures and other promotional information based on past purchases. On paper it had all looked exciting.

Barbara had shown the proposal to her own boss, the VP of marketing, who had been impressed with the volume of sales the project promised. He'd been too busy to look closely at the proposal, but Mario trusted that Barbara had reviewed the plan carefully before submitting it to him. So he decided to put it on the agenda for the next senior management meeting. Mario suggested that Barbara bring her team to the meeting.

An Almost-Shelved Project

The group was delighted with the chance to be present when their idea would be discussed. Their faces were all smiles as they saw the CEO read through the two-page proposal. Several senior managers' head began to nod. It was looking as if the idea would get the group's stamp of approval when Bert Vener spoke up. Bert was VP of systems.

"I have a major concern with the campaign," he told Barbara and her group. "When I first came to this company about two years ago, you told me that our customer records weren't always accurate. We have been trying to get approval for a new database system to remedy the problem, but we haven't been able to get the funding. This proposal doesn't take into consideration the accuracy of the data we currently have. Nor does it include the cost of a new data system, which we really would need for the kind of saturated mailing campaign being proposed."

The room was suddenly silent. Barbara had known about the problem, but in her enthusiasm over the team's projections she had forgotten about the inadequacy of the firm's customer records. Obviously, so had the team leader and members of the team.

Fortunately for Barbara and her team, Bert was on their side. Rather than criticize the idea, he told the group how much he liked the premise behind it. "Could we go back a step and rethink the project and propose, instead, purchase of the database?" he asked.

"It will position us to undertake the proposed mailing campaigns a year from now," he continued. "I'd be delighted to work with Barbara and Sally, the team's leader, and the team to put together cost estimates on the new database."

Barbara's embarrassing moment was salvaged, but the experience, she later told me, has taught her something about mentoring. "Mentoring a group doesn't mean you give up responsibility for the final results. I thought well of Sally. And I still do. But I should have followed up on her work and that of the team before letting the group submit its recommendations to senior management. I was too caught up in its proposal to look objectively at the idea."

Thanking the Group for Its Efforts

Whatever the results of the team effort—whether its recommendations are approved or not—you, as team mentor, should hold a wrap-up meeting to recognize the contribution of the team. Not only the work of the leader should be acknowledged. Every member should be personally thanked by you for their efforts. If you can't provide monetary awards to the members, at the very least you should send a memo to each for placement in his or her personnel file recognizing the contribution made to the team effort. If you can, invite the group to lunch for a celebration. If you chose team members well, these people are very likely the same individuals you would want to be part of the next project you mentor. You want to give them reason to say yes when you ask them again to work on a project for you.

Chapter 12

Mentoring Traps and How to Avoid Them

Not all mentoring efforts work out as planned. Like all human relationships, they have their ups and their downs. Fortunately, some of the downs, or traps, can be prevented. Just as forewarned is forearmed in coaching and counseling, so too is it with mentoring. You can maximize the benefits of mentoring top talent and avoid potential problems by an awareness of the kinds of problems that can arise in mentoring.

Breaking Up: When It's Time for the Mentee to Move On

Interestingly, one major mentoring trap is the belief of the mentor that he can't end the relationship, that only the mentee can do that. Not so.

There are several reasons why you might want to end the mentoring relationship, including the possibility that the top performer has outgrown you. Yes, it is possible for you to mentor a talented employee to the point where she needs challenges that you can't offer. Then you may want to recommend that the top employee find another mentor, maybe a manager with a growing department in which opportunities for promotion for your talented mentee might arise.

It might seem that you are making an unnecessary sacrifice,

but consider the reality. If your mentee is as bright and as hard-working as you believe, he probably feels a little restless. He may be thinking of career opportunities outside your organization. Better to keep him with your organization. And while you may lose an outstanding employee, you could find that department productivity and morale increase as staff members see what your efforts on their coworker's behalf have brought.

Needless to say, it is easier to end mentoring relationships built on a few brief meetings than it is to write "finis" to a long-term relationship with an exceptional staff member with whom you have probably built good rapport. In a short relationship, you can continue to show interest but also look for opportunities for her to meet with and seek answers from others in the organization. In time, you will find that the employee comes to you for help less frequently.

But you will have to explain your decision to end a mentorship with your top performer. The employee needs to know why you feel you can no longer continue to contribute to his career advancement. That you're too busy only sends a message to the mentee that he is not as important as you initially made him believe he was. It will only demotivate him and lower his level of performance, whereas you entered into the mentoring arrangement to further increase this talented employee's contribution to the department or company as a whole.

Point out those developmental gaps that the employee still has and the skills that a new mentor must have to help close them—areas in which you are not expert. Then, together with your staff member, develop a list of prospective new mentors that have these strengths. If a mentee has the talents that attracted you in the first place, it should be possible for you to find another mentor for him or for the mentee to locate one for himself.

Even though you end the mentorship with a staff member or other mentee, you should make clear to the employee that your door is always open for those times that the employee needs help—the same as it is for any employee.

When Mentoring Hurts Rather Than Helps

What kinds of mentorship problems should cause you to dissolve the relationship? Some mentors have found that mentoring can inhibit their employee's development rather than support it. The talented employee becomes so dependent on her managerial mentor that there is actually a decline in performance. First, rather than try to resolve problems on her own, the mentee continually runs to her mentor for help. But, worse, rather than begin to build her own network of contacts, this talented employee has become dependent on you to use your network of contacts both within and outside the organization.

Your employee will be giving so much attention to the mentorship that she won't be developing connections with others important to her success, and perhaps even focusing more on the mentorship than on her routine work.

Evidence of this is cause to end the mentoring relationship. Overdependence on a mentor is a major trap, and the only way it can be addressed is by severing the relationship as soon as there is proof of its existence.

After all, the purpose of mentoring a top talent is to increase individual or organization effectiveness. Your mentee can become complacent unless you take action. Which is to take that little chick you put under your wing and kick her out of the nest.

Personality Conflicts

Another reason for ending a mentorship, even with a talented staff member, is that you just don't like the person. You offered help when the employee first joined your team, but you have since found that you are always at odds with this person. Yes, he is a hard worker and very talented. But it's hard enough being objective about this person as his supervisor; your extraordinary mentoring sessions with him are only turning into debates that seem to overflow into the workplace. Time spent with this individual could more productively be spent with another and equally talented employee who would be more willing to listen to your feedback.

Let the person know that you want to see him grow in the job and that you will help with job-related problems he might encounter, but suggest more suitable candidates as mentor for this individual.

Avoid such a situation in the future by waiting through a get-acquainted period before extending an offer to be available to mentor a new hire.

A Mentee With an Achilles' Heel

Still another reason to get out of a mentorship is if you find after time with the mentee that she is unable to develop the new skills important to her career advancement. Generally, it's not a matter of the person developing new abilities or knowledge but rather one of acquiring political savvy or adapting to the corporate culture. This was the problem with one mentee, her mentor told me.

Sara had done a terrific job on a business proposal. Which was why Sal offered to mentor her; he envisioned her working with him on numerous projects.

Sal knew that Sara came from a more traditionally structured organization, but he didn't think she would have any difficulty working on the team-based initiatives he often became involved in. Not so. Rather than work with him on these projects, Sara buried herself behind papers stacked two feet high on her desk. When she wasn't memoing someone (on paper, although the company had e-mail), she was issuing reports that no one was reading.

Sal tried hard to get her to change her work style but to no avail. She was deaf to his pleas to involve herself in the team initiatives. He ultimately decided to devote his time to another individual whose work habits were more culturally in tune with his own work and the organization's new approach to the work.

Clearly Sal and Sara were a mentoring mismatch. Since Sal's organization was moving toward a team-based structure, Sara was probably a hiring mistake to begin with.

Before sharing some mentoring problems that are remedial, let me address two other mentoring situations that can create problems. Of these, I would agree with Harry Truman, that "If you can't stand the heat. . . ."

Cross-Gender Mentoring

Rumors can arise if you are a male manager and you choose to mentor a female employee. Likewise, if you are a female manager and choose to mentor a male employee. The likelihood of a sexual relationship between a manager mentor and an employee mentee can easily become a subject of discussion on a corporate grapevine, regardless of the parties' personal or professional reputations. One manager was warned by his boss that he might not get a promotion he clearly had earned because of his mentoring relationship with a female staff member, despite her fine professional reputation. The office rumor mill said that he was spending so much time with the young woman that they had to be having an affair. Which they weren't.

The manager was happily married. The woman wasn't married, but she was engaged. Their meetings were always in his office. Neither had ever been the source of office gossip in the past. Yet the manager had to choose between continuing to help his administrative assistant achieve her goal of becoming a CPA or ensuring his promotion.

The press recently contacted me on this very issue. One question asked: Should a female mentee always keep the door open while being counseled by a male mentor? My reply at the time: No woman should find herself in a mentoring situation with a male in which she feels she has to keep the door open to protect either herself or her reputation. But in retrospect, that reply was too simplistic.

Cross-gender mentoring can be open to misunderstanding in today's sexually conscious world. Those who enter into it need to be prepared to find that some people, often jealous of the special attention the mentee is getting, may spread rumors. Should you find yourself in such a situation, the good news is that the gossip mongers usually get bored when they see no fire and move on, looking for other signs of smoke.

Despite his boss's warnings, the VP of finance in our story got his promotion, although he continued to help his assistant advance in her career. Rather than dissolve the mentorship, he extended it to include another staff member—another woman—who took his job when the manager moved up. As for the administrative assistant, she received her degree in accounting, got married, and now works for a tax return processing company.

Reaching Down Below

An equally awkward situation occurs when you mentor a subordinate of one of your direct reports. Don't say you would never think of it. It could happen. Maybe one of your direct reports has an employee who has lots of potential. If you decide to mentor that individual, recognize the impact that it will have not only on your new mentee's relationship with his boss but on your relationship with your direct report.

Unless you see the mentorship as a short-term step before promoting the individual to the spot you have in mind, meet with your direct report and discuss his mentoring the individual. Such involvement will clarify the roles and responsibilities of everyone involved in the mentoring relationship.

Otherwise, any problems between the mentee and boss will become exacerbated as the mentee reaches out to you to resolve the problems. And new problems can arise between you and the boss as the boss sees himself losing control over his own direct report.

Further Problems in Mentoring

So far, I've identified problems that might cause you to dissolve the mentorship and situations that could create problems outside the relationship. Now let me discuss some mentorship problems that are remedial.

Failure to Live Up to Expectations

Either mentor or mentee, or both, may be guilty of this. You may have selected among your staff members a top performer whom you thought you could make into a project leader or an informal assistant to you, but the person hasn't lived up to your expectations. That potential may still be evident to you, but the employee hasn't been following any of the developmental suggestions you have made to her. The employee might have misunderstood your offer to be available to provide feedback, or to broker, or to serve as an advocate; instead, she might have interpreted it as a fast track to advancement without the need for any further effort on her part to develop the competencies you originally saw in her.

If this is the case, then it is time to make clear to the individual that the extra effort you are making for her in the form of mentoring has a price, and that is increased performance, development of new skills or abilities, leadership of a team effort, or whatever developmental goals you both agreed on.

You too could be letting down the partnership. Maybe you meant it when you told your staff member that you would be accessible any time he needed help. But now you find that your calendar is too full to accommodate the time your employee mentee needs. Rescheduled meetings over time suggest to him that he is a low priority for you. This is a frequent problem for managers who agree to mentor an employee.

Too often, they assume that initiating the relationship is more than sustaining it. Not so. Expressing one's intention to mentor someone is, perhaps, at most only 10 percent of building the partnership; the day-to-day effort—the ongoing communication and support—is the other 90 percent.

When that continuous effort isn't forthcoming, no matter what your assertions about how important the employee and his career are to you, the greater the likelihood is that the protégé will become frustrated. He will become disenchanted about the relationship, even question your motives, maybe even doubt his own worth.

You have two options here. You can seek out someone else to mentor your employee, perhaps a peer who has more time than you do right now. Or you can find the time, maybe meet during lunch, if your calendar is so busy that you can't meet in your office during the workday. Or suggest that you and the employee meet before the start of the workday or after everyone else has left.

One warning: Some mentees may have an expectation beyond reality as to your availability. So it is best to be clear at the beginning about how much time each month you can devote to the individual. Too much time, and the mentee can become too dependent on you. Or you may both find yourselves sitting together in the office with nothing to talk about but your wife's new job or the mentee's child's report card.

If you can, commit your calendar ahead of time to meeting with the mentee to ensure that you always have the agreed upon time available.

Communication or Stylistic Managerial Weaknesses

Some managers lack the communication or managerial styles critical to mentoring. For instance, a manager may criticize, rather than listen, or she may provide the mentee with answers rather than risk the mentee making a mistake, or she may become more than an advocate for the mentee, by assuming the role of press agent, perhaps selling the mentee for a team leader role, not because this person is right for the assignment or has done a good job in similar positions but largely because of the relationship between the mentor and the individual.

WHEN ADVICE BECOMES CRITICISM

To understand the impact that mentor behavior can have on the relationship, consider the mentorship between Glenda and her staff member Martha. Martha was one of Glenda's top engineers. Twice monthly Glenda met with Martha to work with her on her interpersonal skills. It was a promise Glenda had made to Martha when she persuaded her to join her division rather than go with a competitive firm.

Martha's division had been downsized, but her technical know-how had caught Glenda's attention in planning discussions that had included Martha and her former boss, Howard. So when Howard's division was dissolved, Glenda immediately had sought out Martha and offered her a slot in her division.

At that time, Martha told her about a job offer she had received from a competitive firm, so Glenda went out of her way to point up the opportunities for advancement in her own area. When Martha mentioned that she was worried about her weakness in interpersonal skills, Glenda had jumped at the opportunity to offer to help Martha if she stayed with the company and agreed to join Glenda's operation. Although the word *mentor* was never mentioned, Glenda's offer encompassed all the roles of a mentor—role model, adviser, broker, and advocate—for the purpose of making Martha more at ease in team situations.

Half a Year Later

Six months have passed. As Glenda promised, she continued to meet with Martha every second week. At these sessions, Glenda shared with her new staff member her own experiences in dealing with others and critiqued Martha's efforts at improving her people skills.

During the first few sessions, Martha seemed receptive to Glenda's suggestions. Since Martha and Glenda both attended several meetings together, Glenda could comment from firsthand observation, not simply listen to Martha describe situations and how she had handled them. Martha had even seemed grateful when Glenda called a break at one meeting Glenda was heading when Martha seemed to be at a loss for words in defending an idea for improving the division's intranet setup.

On the other hand, Martha showed little interest after the fact in hearing Glenda's suggestions for how Martha could have better handled the situation. Or how embarrassed Glenda had felt for Martha. "I never found myself in such a bind," she had told Martha. "You really have a problem communicating with people. But don't worry. We'll find some way to help you."

Martha at this point sometimes seemed to go out of her way to do just the opposite of what Glenda told her to do at their mentoring meetings.

A Helping Hand From Howard . . .

No longer delighted with Glenda's offer to help, Martha had now become visibly angry about having to give up her lunch hours to meet with Glenda. It was clear to Glenda that something was wrong. So when she spotted Howard in the hallway, she asked him to come to her office to talk. When his division had been eliminated, Howard had been relocated to the company's Houston office.

"What's up?" Howard asked as he closed Glenda's office door. "I was glad to see that you were able to keep Martha. I've seen your operating numbers, and I bet some of those savings were due to her systems improvements. That woman is a technical genius."

"If she could only be as good working with other people," Glenda said.

"Martha isn't comfortable with people; she never was. I know. But it shouldn't be affecting her work. In fact, she's probably just as happy tinkering with computers, off by herself."

Glenda decided to tell Howard about her promise to Martha.

"I'm surprised she admitted her weakness about working with others, but I'm delighted that she recognizes it as a weakness," Howard observed. "But if she could improve her people skills, she would be in line for a team leadership or supervisory position."

"That's what I had in mind," Glenda continued. "But the time I am spending with her isn't making any change in her performance. In fact, she seems even more standoffish with others."

Howard then listened as Glenda described how she had instructed Martha in how to behave with the other members of the team. "I've reviewed what she has done wrong after each meeting, and I've told her how I used to handle such situations in the past. Yet she doesn't seem to change."

... And a Finger on the Problem

Howard was silent for a moment. "I hate to say this, but the problem may be as much with your handling of the problem as with Martha's receptivity to a very sensitive subject."

"What do you mean?" Glenda asked, sincerely interested in Howard's view of the situation. "I thought I was giving Martha constructive criticism."

"There is no such thing," Howard said. "The two words just don't belong together when you are talking about giving an employee feedback to help her deal with an obstacle to career advancement. You may have thought you were helping to build her up—that's the constructive part—but all that the criticism has really been doing, from what you say, is tearing her down. From my own experience as a supervisor and manager, I know that employees don't listen if you give them feedback in the form of criticism.

"By criticizing Martha all the time about her work with others and always advising her about a better way or, worse still, coming to her rescue," Howard continued, "you are telling Martha that you think she's hopeless in dealing with people. You aren't building her self-confidence, you're destroying what little self-confidence she had about working with others. And she's resentful because she thought you were a friend. Instead, you've become her toughest critic."

Glenda thought for a moment. After her first meeting with Martha, Glenda had to admit, she had assumed a more directive approach with Martha. Rather than ask a series of questions to help Martha identify for herself how she might better have handled situations, Glenda had jumped in with advice and lectures. In considering the situation, Glenda realized she needed to go back to the consultative approach she had used earlier if she was to rebuild her previous rapport with Martha.

Giving advice, extricating the mentee from a potentially embarrassing situation, and focusing on the "how to" rather than the reason why something should be done might seem to be faster ways to mentor an employee, but these behaviors do little to build the individual's self-confidence. At a point when you, as mentor, might want to empower your employee mentee, instead you wind up disempowering her.

Unrealistic Developmental Goals

Glenda may also have had an unrealistic expectation about how quickly Martha could learn how to interact more effectively with people.

Actually, this is a problem that can go both ways. While a mentor may demand more of the mentee over a shorter time than she is capable of, so too may a mentee expect more, besides time, of the mentor than she has the ability or willingness to provide. For instance, a mentee may expect the mentor to protect him from organizational pressures, perhaps even a downsizing. But the mentor may be unaware of the political problems her mentee is experiencing or, in the case of a potential layoff, she may lack the clout to save the mentee from the corporate ax.

Whatever the misunderstandings, they can cause hostility to grow between the mentor and mentee. The mentor may have set goals with the mentee, and the two may have much in common, but the mentor can become an easy target if a promotion that the mentee expected isn't forthcoming or the mentee blames the mentor for a mistake, even though the mentee made it himself. While the goal was to boost the mentee's performance, the emotion between the two can affect the mentee's performance and even cause it to decline.

Because such problems can arise, you have to be very specific in discussions with a prospective mentee about what you will provide. This is particularly the case when mentoring a staff member. The employee shouldn't feel that he will be favored over other staff members because of your extraordinary relationship.

Unfair Treatment by the Mentor

The opposite of a mentor who believes that a mentee can do no wrong is the one for whom a mentee can do no right, with the mentee receiving harsher feedback than coworkers do for the same mistakes. However, even a mentee who has always seemed to be receiving favorable treatment from his mentor can suddenly find himself getting the short end of the stick, as Carl had the misfortune to learn.

The Star Who Was Unfairly Eclipsed

Carl, now a manufacturing VP for an auto company, told me that he had actually lost a promotion because he was a manager's mentee. The manager, Jack, was asked his opinion of employees Carl and Tony, who were candidates for promotion to head a department. Jack had chosen Carl to mentor because he worked so hard and had come up with some good ideas to reduce costs. Yet Jack recommended Tony for the promotion, even though he had spent numerous lunches with Carl griping about Tony.

"I had been with the company for about seven years," Carl recalled. "Tony had been with us for less than a year. Our boss, Jack, who a year or so before had offered to help me move up by teaching me to 'think more strategically with my crew,' had hired Tony. But only a few weeks later he admitted to me that he thought he had made a mistake.

"Each time Jack and I met for lunch," Carl went on, "he would spend the first thirty or forty-five minutes on new strategic initiatives that my team and I could support, and then the remaining thirty minutes on Tony's mistakes. Tony didn't 'accept responsibility for his crew's mistakes,' or he allowed problems 'to get out of hand because he didn't address them early on,' or he and his team had isolated themselves from the division because Tony 'doesn't collaborate with the rest of the team leaders.'

"I knew that Jack would have influence on the promotion, and I admit I expected him to go to bat for me," Carl said. "So it came as a real shock to hear that, when asked for his recommendation, he suggested Tony for the job.

"I didn't ask him why he hadn't recommended me but at our next meeting it became clear to me why he had acted as he had. Jack was afraid that he might be accused of showing favoritism if he supported me for the position. But instead of not saying anything, he focused on all the weaknesses we had discussed over lunch.

"I had considered our discussions confidential, so I was especially upset that Jack had shared with Dave the litany of errors I had made over seven years."

Clearly, Jack had violated the confidentiality that is key to a mentoring relationship. But his fears about being accused of favoritism also caused him to be unfair to the talented superstar on his team. Parenthetically, being passed over for promotion prompted Carl to leave the firm and move up to manager with another firm.

Botton line: You, as a mentor, may be accused of showing favoritism. The only defense you have is evidence that the person you are mentoring is worthy of the time and talent you give to his or her professional development.

Jealousy on the Part of Other Staff Members

A mentee can become the object of jealousy of coworkers, particularly when the mentoring is conducted outside a structured program. Those without mentors may feel that those who are being mentored are getting special treatment. If you sense jealousy, you can address it by being as accessible to other staff members as you are to your mentee. You should also alert the mentee not to aggravate the situation by flaunting his or her new association with you.

Identifying Problems

If you suspect that there is a problem in your mentoring relationship, you may want to use this list of ten questions to set matters straight:

1. Are we addressing your needs?
2. Do you feel a sense of satisfaction from our ongoing meetings?
3. Do you have expectations that are not being met?
4. What could be done to improve our conversations?
5. Do you feel that we are spending more time together than you now need?
6. Are there some special issues that we should put on the table and address [for example, the likelihood of co-worker jealousies, ethnic or cross-gender communication problems, or mistaken impressions about the relationship]?
7. Do you see the same need for my help as you did originally?
8. If we have achieved our initial goals, what would be the next goals?
9. Am I still the person to help you reach your next level of accomplishments?
10. Is there someone else within the organization who would be a more appropriate mentor at this stage in your development?

The discussion may identify problems with the current relationship, but if they are ones that the mentee believes are remediable, she may want to continue to come to you for career advice and developmental help. The decision then falls on you to decide whether to try to improve the situation or to discontinue the relationship.

Under these circumstances you may want to walk away, but you owe it to the staff member to make an effort to revitalize the mentorship. This includes a willingness to accept responsibility for the problems that still exist.

But you must also demand the same honesty and responsiveness from your protégé.

Assuming you identify changes that you believe will turn the situation around, give the partnership a month. Then ask the same ten questions once again. If there has been no change, then you are justified in ending the relationship.

Epilogue

Everyone admires the manager who has a great staff of employees. His workers are both productive and cooperative. There are even one or two superstars in the department or work team. Guess what? That manager could be you as you apply the information in this book to your working relationships with your employees.

If there is one thought you should take away from reading this book, it is this: People problems, whatever their nature or level of seriousness, shouldn't be ignored. Avoidance is the fastest way to make an employee situation get worse, even allow it to become infectious, expanding beyond the single worker to encompass an entire department. The situation can grow so large that it can hinder your relationship not only with the rest of the staff but also with your own boss and other managers, and even bring you to the attention of senior management for all the wrong reasons.

Because it is repeated so frequently, the phrase "People are our most important asset" may seem only like rhetoric. Certainly the behavior of some companies has caused many employees and even managers to regard the statement as nothing more than corporate propaganda. But it is a fact of business life, and as a manager, your role is to increase the worth of that human capital. Consider the impact that competent, highly motivated employees could have on achieving your department's mission and its contribution to the bigger corporate mission and your organization's strategic intent—not to mention your career.

Admittedly, you're very busy. And people situations can be tricky. But the kind of attention to people problems that this book proposes should take not more than 10 percent of your time. On the other hand, failure to allocate that 10 percent when you first see a performance problem can cost you 50 percent or more of your time if the problem grows beyond coaching or mentoring to counseling. At best, you will have to pick up the slack from an unproductive employee. If the problem continues, you will find yourself taking time away from bottom-line assignments to justify the individual's termination. And if you have failed to be upfront with the worker all along, you may find yourself preoccupied with fear about a lawsuit brought by the disgruntled employee whom you could have salvaged with some effort earlier on.

Not responding at the first signs of a problem can allow enough time for a small molehill of a people problem to grow into a mountain that you professionally never get over. Better to demonstrate your belief in the phrase "People are our most important asset" by coaching all your employees, counseling your poorer performers in order to turn their behavior around, and mentoring your superstars to keep them shining than to stand with your peers and look covetously at those managers with high-performing teams who are recognized and rewarded by senior management for all the right reasons. That's the WIIFM (What's In It For Me) in taking action to boost employee performance when you become aware of the need.

Aside from the personal pride you will take in building and then overseeing a highly productive work group, you will have the knowledge that your team's successful track record is reflecting well on you. And looking down, those at the next level above you can see it.

Index